THE

PIVOT

YEAR

365 DAYS TO BECOME THE PERSON YOU TRULY WANT TO BE

BRIANNA WIEST

THOUGHT
CATALOG
Books

THOUGHTCATALOG.COM

INTRODUCTION

I hope this is the year you change your life.

Not in the superficial way. Not in the way of moving things around on the surface and wondering why nothing feels much different underneath. Not in the way of conformity. Not in the way that aligns you most closely with all of the traditional emblems of success, the ones that leave you smiling beside your accomplishments but feeling so pinched with guilt and regret.

I hope this is the year you change your life in the ways you have always secretly wanted to. The year you discover those quiet dreams that have lingered for so long are actually echoes of parallel lives, sister stories asking you to tell them, to leap toward them, to move them out of your mind and into a touchable, physical reality.

I hope that this is the year that you change your life in only the way you can, with the power only you have. I can't do it for you. The words can't do it for you. They can only encourage and guide you like an old friend, a message from far beyond and deep within. I hope you focus more on what you feel between the lines than what you see on the pages. I hope each day makes you take pause and contemplate what invisible, third door of possibility you may have missed. I hope you are not afraid to go inward, the space from which your entire life is born.

I hope that this is the year you stop dancing around the perimeter of who you intended to be, of what you came here to do. I hope that this is the year you learn to defy what's reasonable and build sense in a world of your own design. I hope that this is the year you discover that the floor does not only hold up if you remain where you are standing—with each step you take, and wherever you may go, it will rise to meet you, as it always has, as it always does.

I hope that this is the year you realize everything—every last thing in your life—will happen with much more ease if it is in alignment with your soul's true intent. I hope this is the year you begin to unearth those truths from inside of you. I hope that this is the year you find the boldest, bravest kind of courage. I hope that this is the year you walk fiercely into the life that was always meant to be yours.

Within you lives a great vision for your life, quieted over time by the world.

It is once again time to listen.
It is once again time to live.

—*Brianna Wiest*

2)(05(2021)

DAY 1

The courage with which you enter today will become the fate that you meet tomorrow. *Will you continue to replay the memories of yesterday, or will you meet the moment and make the most of what is in front of you now?* Not so that you might force your will upon your fate, but arrive fully into each moment as it's presented to you. Not to build a clean, one-line story, but to create a mosaic of experience—ever-forming, ever-evolving, ever-unfolding, as what's within unravels into reality, revealing at last the fragment of the universe that came to be known through you at this exact time, in this exact place, in this exact form. You are exactly where you need to be. This is the perfect day to start your life again.

DAY 2

There is great power in not knowing. Not knowing what is next, not knowing what to decide, not knowing how you will make it to where you know you want and need to be. Every given moment contains within it doorways of opportunity, and when you choose to walk through one, you make realities available to you that were once invisible. When you do not know what is next, you enter the realm of infinite potential. Instead of trying to plan your life so safely and so succinctly, you can begin to plan for the moment, the joy, the journey. Instead of living on autopilot, you can learn how to continuously meet the ever-changing, ever-possible *now*. When you finally admit that you do not know what is next, you enter the golden vortex—the space between everything you know you're meant for and anything you had previously imagined to be.

DAY 3

One day you will realize that happiness is not what your house looks like, but how you love the people within its walls. Happiness is not finding success by a certain time, but finding something you love so much time itself seems to disappear. Happiness is not thinking you have earned the world's approval, but waking up each day and feeling so at peace within your own skin, quietly anticipating the day ahead, unconcerned with how you are perceived. Happiness is not having the best of everything, but the ability to make the best of anything. Happiness is knowing you are doing what you can with what you were given. Happiness is not something that comes to you when every problem is solved and all things are perfectly in place, but in the shining silver linings that remind us the light of day is always there, if you slow down enough to notice.

26105120

DAY 4

Self-protection is learning how to take a pause between what you feel and how you react. When there is no awareness between what you perceive and the way that you respond, anything can control you. *Practice the pause.* Widen the space between what you sense and what you do about it. Decide what's worth your energy, because what you engage with is what you empower.

DAY 5

There are two rivers running through us at all times, one that carries all the voices of the world, and the other, a single voice that stands alone—the voice of our inner guide. The first river is so strong, steady, and constant with its instruction, guidance, and forewarning; most of us live mindlessly being pulled to each milestone, each thing we were told to reach for, to move toward, to achieve. Eventually, we look down and realize our hands are empty. Our lives were woven together by a storyline we didn't write. As we lose sight of our inner compass, a fog is cast over our awareness of the moment. We become saddled with confusion, indecision and uncertainty. We become incapable of leading ourselves because the two rivers are shouting over one another, tempting us with virtues, and repelling us with vices. Over time, we become consumed by the stiffness of trying to be what we are told, existing in contrast to the soft, effervescent truth living deep inside. Despite how loud that first river can become, we can always hear the quiet call of the second. Our lives begin the day we choose to follow our inner knowing, even while hearing, at times heeding, the collective knowledge of the first. The first realization of wisdom is the recognition that there is truth fragmented everywhere, and to delineate the two rivers into wholly good and wholly bad is to deprive ourselves of the depth and beauty that our hearts are truly trying to bring about. The journey is not about abandoning one in favor of the other, but knowing when it is time to listen, to hear, and to follow each.

D A Y   6

You cannot desire what you do not already contain. Desire is a projection outward that is proportionate to potential inward. There are so many possibilities within this world, so many things to hope for and to aspire to. There are so very many things one could want, and yet, it is a very specific vision that awakens you on the inside. There are very few things that excite you in a way that makes you nearly uncomfortable with your wanting of them. Desire is so integral to who you are, it is part of you even if you are not conscious of it—even when your ego chooses to shield you from your awareness of it. What you are waiting on is your own willingness to accept the mountain you must climb in order to pull those desires out of the deepest parts of you and create them in the world you already inhabit.

DAY 7

Maybe you don't need to find more energy, maybe you just need to find a dream that makes you actually want to get up in the morning. Maybe you need to find something that gives back more than it takes. Maybe you need to stop trying to be good at the hundred things that do not light up your soul, and finally choose the one that does—the one that asks you to risk, to lay your heart bare, to try again, even though you're scared. You're not failing because you're not motivated. You're not supposed to get far on a path that was never yours to walk.

D A Y   8

You may believe that living life to the fullest is seeing every country in the world and quitting your job on a whim and falling recklessly in love, but it's really just knowing how to be where your feet are. It's learning how to take care of yourself, how to make a home within your own skin. It's learning how to build a simple life you are proud of. A life most fully lived is not always composed of the things that rock you awake, but those that slowly assure you it's okay to slow down. That you don't always have to prove yourself. That you don't need to fight forever, or constantly want more. That it's okay for things to be just as they are. Little by little, you will begin to see that life can only grow outward in proportion to how stable it is inward—that if the joy is not in the little things first, the big things won't fully find us.

DAY 9

Whatever pain you think you are in right now cannot begin to compare to the peace that will one day come over you. It cannot begin to compare to the joy that you will one day know. You will fall in love with life again, and it will be better than it was before, because you will become a different person. You will become someone who is more capable of appreciating what matters, who will not be as reckless with their choices, who can no longer be so easily swayed or mindlessly trusting. You will require a new level of integrity within your life, which will transpire into better boundaries and a more stable foundation. You will strengthen in the most unexpected ways, and from that, your happiness will be even more sincere, even more apparent. This will not happen overnight, though it will seem like it did in retrospect. Like the changing of a season, everything shifts slowly until all of a sudden, you are standing firmly in the after, in all you feared would never come. You're through it, but you're different, because something also moved through you and cleared out what you didn't even realize was standing in the way.

DAY 10

The journey is not how you place down what's weighing on you, but how you learn to stop picking it up. Not when you decide to stop, but the strength of your resolve not to begin again—with the habits, the people, the thoughts, the behaviors that you know can only lead to your own self-destruction. It's how you release your familiar unhappiness, how you decide you've outgrown the emotional crutches that have soothed you and distracted you and held you when you most needed it. How you move forward is what you begin to reach for in their place.

D A Y 11

You do not have to be grateful for everything in your life. You do not have to be grateful for what you survived, for what you didn't know, for the lessons learned too hard. You do not have to be grateful for the unfairness, to live in a world that does not value dignity the way that it should, a world that has lost its soul. But even in the midst of the storm, when you stumble upon a glimmer of appreciation, I hope you will hold onto that. I hope you will know that it is as real as anything else. I hope you will offer it as much attention as you can give. I hope you will remember that silver linings foretell of the light of day that will come. I hope you will know that just because you are not grateful for all of it doesn't mean you aren't grateful for any of it. I hope you will allow yourself to contain more than one truth—that not every phase of your life will tell the same story. That not every piece of this existence will flow congruently to the last. That more is possible, even if the past did not show you that it is. That our greatest dreams and our deepest fears may coexist, and the existence of one does not negate or lessen the other. That the very moment that you honor where you are with complete surrender, you open to the next experience life wants to offer.

D A Y   1 2

Heal your relationship to the now, to the moment, to the liminal space in which your eyes can contract and see fear, or expand and realize that you are one particle in this massive daydream, and without you the fabric of the world would not hold the way it does. Release yourself into the dreamscape, and follow your heart's deepest calling, as it is leading you to the actions that will continue to weave your life into the story of humanity. Without you being here, nothing—not one single thing—would be precisely the same. You are an integral, irreplaceable thing. You came here to do what only you can.

DAY 13

You tell life *what* you want, and life tells you *how* to get it. When you ask for soulmate love, you must listen if life says, *but not with them*. When you ask for prosperity, you must listen if life says, *but not like this*. When you ask for belonging, you must listen if life says, *but not here*. What feels on the surface like rejection is often redirection. When you ask for a big life, you cannot keep fighting for a smaller one to stay.

D A Y 1 4

Move toward the people who expand your perimeter of possibility, who believe in your potential just a little bit more than your reality. Move toward the people who remind you of the person you know you're meant to be, the ones who stretch your soul and make you feel something real. Move toward the people who remind you of what you contain, who help you fall a little more in love with life. Move toward the people who energize you more than they drain you. These little signs are not so little—they are the markers of our soulmates, in all the forms they come.

DAY 15

Declare: *I will no longer participate in my own suffering.* If I have not one other friend in this world, I will be my own most loyal companion. I will not turn my back on myself. If I am loved by a dozen and not one, I will not focus undue attention on gaining the love of that one. I will speak to myself with compassion. I will not spend my life engaging in things that can only bring about my own unhappiness. From this moment on, I am on my own side.

DAY 16

You may fear the quiet times in your life, when your soul goes through a winter. However, it's often those same times when the most profound and human work of all is being completed. Be still. Do nothing. It is both the quiet and the noise that writes the symphony, the blank canvas and the paint that makes the picture, the rest and the movement that gives you the wisdom, insight and clarity to press forward more boldly than ever before.

DAY 17

Maybe you should trust the missed connections, the calls gone unanswered, the opportunities that had every reason to work out but didn't. Maybe you should trust in the small signs before they become big ones. Maybe you should trust those tiny contractions, the nights that exhaust you and the people who don't see you and the places that make you feel that subtle uneasiness. Maybe you should learn to trust in what passes you by so you'll begin to trust in what lands right in front of you. Maybe you should trust that in what isn't working, because it might be trying to guide you to what will.

DAY 18

Every hour is a new beginning—you just don't realize it until you remember that every soul-shifting, life-changing experience you have happens in an otherwise ordinary day. In an instant, you meet a moment that changes your world forever. You find the job, you book the flight, you sign the papers, you choose to make the change that changes it all. Chapters of great transformation often feel like they carry on forever, but the truth is that they are often gardens that grow from tiny seeds that you've been planting for a very long time.

DAY 19

What is meant for you will arrive in your life and it will remain in your life. What did not transpire was not meant to; the end of that journey would not have led you somewhere you would have wanted or needed to be. If you are really honest with yourself, you know this on the inside. There were so many signs that you willingly brushed over in the heat of blind hope. If you spend your life fixated on the might-have-beens, you miss out on the steady currents that have carried you all this way. Notice what stays. Notice what is constant. Notice what perseveres. These are the things that the song of your life will be composed of.

DAY 20

Other people will see you the way they intend to. In the same way you have put the people you admire on pedestals and glossed over all the unseemly aspects of another human being you were hellbent on trying to love; in the same way that the souls closest to you seem the most beautiful and most easily forgivable; in the same way that you most understand the perspective of the people whose journeys you have witnessed from the beginning, whose shoes you can imagine yourself in; other people see you the way they need to and intend to. What matters, in the end, is the way you intend to see yourself.

DAY 21

Nurture and engage in the most stunning aspects of yourself, give the majority of your time to your greatest strengths. You are not here to simply compensate for your weaknesses, to level yourself out in every possible direction. You are not here to grow the parts of you that were never destined to come fully into form.

DAY 22

You have overcome every single thing that has been un-expected, that has been heart-wrenching, that has not gone your way. You have built a life within the complete unknown, you have reconstructed a new version of yourself from the pieces of what you thought would be. You have always contained within yourself the remarkable strength of the human spirit, and no matter what tomorrow will bring, you will carry that power into it, too.

DAY 23

Kindness is evidence of impenetrable strength. It is the willingness to stay soft in a world that tries to harden you at every corner. It is the ability to absorb your own emotions and diffuse them, to decide what you want to act on and what you want to put back out into the world, regardless of what the world has put you through. Kind people are not just good, they are heroes in their own ways. Their ability to not reciprocate unkindness to a world that often deserves it makes them catalysts for the deepest healing to occur.

DAY 24

You are the peace between the highs and the lows, the sky that rests forever behind whatever storms may form and release themselves in time. You'll always return to what you really are, you will always come back to your truth. If there is anything greater than happiness, it is coming to this realization and living with this knowledge. You are all that is steady and safe within you.

14/06/2022

DAY 25

I hope you learn to live in a way that makes you glad to be alive. Not glad for your elevator speech, your accolades, or what you believe the world sees you as. Not where you are glad for all that you might do one day, but the beauty with which you experience the smallest and most unassuming of things. I hope you learn to live in a way that makes you excited for the day ahead, for whatever it is you are meant to do with this period of time, with this corner of the world, with this one body and life that is yours. I hope you learn to experience living, instead of just imagining how your life is seen. I hope you learn to feel it, with everything inside you. I hope you learn to be alive.

15/06/200

DAY 26

Finding yourself also requires losing who you once thought yourself to be. Cultivating the deepest and most lasting forms of inspiration often requires the most rote kind of consistency. Figuring out what's right for you is acknowledging that different things are right at different times—alignment shifts as you do. Healing is often a process of being able to hold and embrace the contrasts of your experience, to embrace them, to let them be.

DAY 27

In an unawakened state, your power is fully externalized. Your faith is placed disproportionately on the systems, regulations, and structures that never had any intention of moving you past where you are now into where you could be. It is often when you reach complete exhaustion and exasperation with this view of the world that you begin to go inward and discover something solvent—the power that's within. As you begin to wake up to that power, you often overuse it. You assume you are a god unto yourself, the tiny particles around which the entire universe will bend and break and reform. You begin to shake off this illusion when you realize that the things you insisted on creating did not turn out as perfectly as you once imagined. You begin to take other people into account, their timing and their needs. You start to see that you cannot see everything, and so begins the true journey of your life, which is the dance between what is yours to handle and what is yours to release. What you must reach for, and what you must allow to come. When it is time to speak, and when it is time to listen. When it is time to teach, and when it is time to learn. When it is time to exert your will and when it is time to surrender to a path far greater than anything you could conceive of prior. This is what it is to live—to understand your free will, and develop the discernment to use it well.

DAY 28

Nothing feels all the way right at the beginning, because nothing is completely familiar at the beginning. What you often don't account for is that your sense of comfort and correctness tends to be rooted in familiarity. The question is not whether something makes you feel immediately as though you're unquestionably fated for it, but whether or not it grows with you. Whether or not it gives you the opportunity to stretch, to change, to become better. That is the true test of what is right—not what instantly falls into place, but what entwines its roots with yours, and allows you to most fully blossom. Not what shows up instantly and unexpectedly, but what stays, what remains through it all.

DAY 29

The things you want to create also want to be created through you. What you are longing to bring into the world is also what the world is longing for you to bring it.

DAY 30

Eventually, you will have to stop pouring yourself into the things that will give nothing back, that take without any intent to give. You will have to stop trying to make yourself fit into places you are no longer meant to be. If you are going to give your energy to anything, give it to what's already working. To the people who already love you, to the things that show potential, to the places that make you feel more alive. Life speaks to us in subtleties, in the smallest possible ways. In the little clicks, the funny coincidences, the ways the ordinary collides into the serendipitous. Sometimes, the quiet whispers are the most accurate ones. The voices of pride and ego and attraction are louder, but they are often devoid of the fullness of truth. Listen for the quiet *yes,* for what gently sprouts, for what grows, and grows.

DAY 31

You are an ocean of unrealized potential. You cannot imagine how deep and how wide your capacity really is unless it's been tested, until you've been moved beyond where you thought your limits were, and have had to redefine them. In this, you find new energy. You find a better rhythm. You rediscover everything you believed you had lost. Our life force can never truly escape us, but it can be withheld until our bodies feel safe enough to begin again. Give yourself the time you need to regulate to your new normal, let yourself witness with each passing day that it is once again safe to exhale, to step outside your comfort zone, to trust in the unknown. Slowly, you will learn to take hold of that wild spirit within you once again, and this time, you will be more focused, and more intentional. You will be more discerning about who and what you allow into your life, into your headspace. You will move forward with more mindfulness. You will begin to see that when your energy is leaking out into a thousand different directions, you cannot fully invest your own potential. You will begin to see that it was never about whether or not you were capable of becoming what you most desire, but that you were simply distracted, unknowingly surrounded by those who infused a sense of disbelief so deeply into your subconscious mind, self-limiting beliefs became the parameters in which you thought you had to experience this world. You will begin to decide what really matters to you, what you actually want to experience while you are alive, and gently, and lovingly, release the rest in time.

DAY 32

You will have to learn how to outgrow some things you love. You will have to learn that some things are right for a time, but not forever. You will have to learn that moving on from them does not diminish the place they held within you, the importance they have to you, or the impact they had on you. You will have to learn that if you are not growing, you are not really living. If you are not moving on from anything, you are not moving toward something. You will have to learn how to let go of some things that are still beautiful, because you know that they are not quite right, because you know that a deeper peace is waiting. The people, places and things that phase in and out of your life come to you for a specific purpose, and once their mission is complete, you are able to move onto the next experience. You will have to learn that the very act of letting go is not a failure, but a signal of completion: one of the truest signs that you are evolving as a human being.

22/06/2011

DAY 33

If you do not know what to do next, it usually isn't because your next step is far out in the distance, but rather right in front of your feet. You are being asked to stop gazing outward and start looking inward. You are being called to rebuild yourself at this exact moment. If you do not know what to do next, it is not because you need to seek more answers, but rather, accept the ones you've already been given. If you do not know what to do next, it's time to learn to be in the answered prayer that is this very day. It's time to learn how to use what you already have, and be as you really are. It's time to stop waiting for some future scenario to bring your dreams into the light, but to dig them out from beneath your fear and begin. Truly begin.

DAY 34

You'll be surprised by how consistently things will show up exactly as you need them to, and not a moment before. When it's time to act, the energy will come. When it's time to make the choice, you'll know what to decide. When it's time to leave, you'll find yourself writing the resignation. *Trust yourself.* You don't have to predict every possible turn of the future, but strengthen your faith in the fact that you will be taken care of no matter where you find yourself along the way.

DAY 35

It's disrupting you because it's trying to move you—to a kinder thought, to a better place, to a deeper knowing. It is trying to open up a piece of your heart that you have closed, to soften you in the places where life has left its harshest scars. It is trying to inspire your forgiveness, to meet others in the moment, as they are now. It is trying to help you stop keeping the past alive by maintaining outdated perceptions, and it's trying to bring you firmly into this moment. It's unnerving to you because it is a messenger, and you have not yet heard what it is trying to say. It is persistent because you need it, even if you don't want it. It's here because it intends to grow you, and it won't pass until you agree to let it stretch you past the tiny confines of a life half-lived.

DAY 36

When we find it too difficult to arrive fully into the present moment, it is almost always because the quiet is telling us something we are not yet ready to hear. The longer we avoid looking honestly at ourselves, the louder our inner worlds will become. When we find the courage to look long enough into the eyes of our demons, they dissolve into crying children, just asking us to set them free.

DAY 37

The healthiest things for you may seem underwhelming if your soul has only known the loudness of continued chaos. Your biggest feelings are not always the most accurate ones.

27106120

DAY 38

On the days when it hurts too much to dream, to hope, to think of anything beyond the line of sight ahead of you—just rest. You were raised in a world that believes your productivity can only exist in outward measure, that the only things worth doing are the ones that others can consume. Your soul cannot be fooled by this, no matter how much your mindset can try to superimpose such rigid beliefs upon you. Eventually, you give way to the guidance of your inner being, the part of you that knows how vital it is to recover, to reintegrate, to reflect, to balance all doing with the simplicity of being. There is nothing wrong with you for needing to take life at your own pace, in your own timing. In fact, there is something emerging from deep within you that is so strong in its conviction that it is making balance your highest priority. Your unwillingness to press forward in outdated ways is not a sign of your noncompliance, but that the spiritual freedom you have cultivated from within is finally beginning to take root.

DAY 39

You are here to carve a new way out of the unknown. You are here to defy what's expected and create a new normal, one where you feel inherently free to not see external challenges as absolute dead-ends, but to discover the quiet resilience you cultivate as you work your way around them. You are here to nurture the feeling a life most fully lived would give you in your chest, not what you imagine it would appear in someone else's eyes.

DAY 40

Instead of thinking of every one of your qualities as fixed, consider that your environment and the structure of your day evoke different emotional states and, with consistency, can begin to appear on the surface as unmovable aspects of who you are. What is happening around you when you are the most peaceful, open-minded, inspired version of yourself? What is happening when you are not? Is it possible that healing could look like making the smallest amendments and seeing how wide their effects might ricochet?

DAY 41

There are a lot of things you can give up on in this life, but love is not one of them. There are a lot of things you can let go of, a lot of things you're allowed to say you were wrong or a little too hopeful about. There are a lot of things you can age out of, phase through, and move on from, but love is not one of them. You have to believe in love up until the very end—real love, true love, honest love. To not give up on love is to be open to how it may come, and when. To not give up on love is to accept that the deepest possible experience of it might not look exactly as you pictured. To not give up on love is to realize that it will not be something that sweeps you off your path, but helps you stand more firmly on your own two feet. It is not something that idealizes an idea of you but does not support the person you are becoming—love is willing to care for you in the most constant, simple, human ways. In the end, love is not something you find one day, it's something you learn to see surrounding you already, it is something you heal yourself into being able to fully receive.

DAY 42

Until you confront the shadow of your own self-disapproval, you will always be gazing out at the world in fear of who might not love you completely, who might draw your awareness to the part of you that already believes you are unworthy of being appreciated, of being fully and truly known. You must find a way to make peace with yourself, even if you cannot madly love every last aspect of who you are. You must come to a place of believing you deserve respect, even if you are still a work in progress. You must learn to see yourself with kinder eyes.

DAY 43

You become who you really are when you start choosing the things that you actually find meaningful and worthwhile. You become who you really are when even the most minor decisions throughout your day reflect your authenticity, when your instinct leads you before your mind interrupts. You become who you really are when you start allowing the brightest parts of you to shine without apology, when you begin to realize there is no substitute for your own love finally flowing through your own life.

DAY 44

We don't need a lot to be happy, but we do need things that are real. We do need things that grip our hearts and enliven us and make us feel like we are here for a reason, here to experience something that could only be touched by a human body, understood by a human mind, loved by a human heart. When we deny ourselves the authentic experience of being alive, we reach for more when what we really want is not to stretch wider, but to go deeper.

04/07/2022

DAY 45

Letting go is not meant to be easy; it is not supposed to be simple to unwind your soul from the things that have captured your mind, your time, and your life for so long. You are not supposed to be able to effortlessly and numbly cut things that were once a part of you out and set them free. You are not supposed to separate yourself from what's most essential within your experience. Your willingness to do so is testimony not to your failure nor your inadequacy but your faith on fire with the knowledge that even still, even here, there is something greater that is waiting to be seen.

DAY 46

In everything you choose, you must first ask: *but what will this do to my soul?* Will it bring me closer to a heavenly state of being, or anchor me into the ache of this world? Will it make me more of the person I was meant to be, or will it distract me from the true work? Will it pay the bills, but bankrupt my being? Will it impress others, but disappoint the child inside me waiting to see what I do with my freedom? Will I arrive at the end of my life proud that I did this? Will I do this now, or will I wait until I am forced to make the decision I already know is right today? Will I spare myself the suffering? Will I have courage?

06|07|2021

DAY 47

Do you know how many perfect moments are unfolding before your very eyes? Do you know how much you already have? Do you know how many quiet nights of peace you have already experienced, how many hearts have loved you, how many people would love to see your name pop up on their phone right now? Do you know how much you matter? Do you know how good you are?

07107/200

DAY 48

It is easy to tell how you are doing in life.

When you go outside, how beautiful is the flower?

That is how you know.

DAY 49

Don't depend on anyone, but learn to rely on the ones you trust. Make your home your safe space. When it feels like nothing is happening, that's when everything is about to happen. Don't get so used to chaos that peace feels like something's wrong. Love is something you build, attraction is something you find. Nobody has everything, but everyone has something—focus on your something. If you really start to pay attention, you will be amazed at what you find.

DAY 50

The space between *no longer* and *not yet* is what defines the pivot periods of our lives. This is the time when we have nothing left to hold onto but also nowhere clearly to land. This is when most people revert back to their oldest and most familiar coping mechanisms, confusing what's known for what's right. If we find the courage to hold our hearts open throughout this process, what we find is that we create an opportunity for miracles to find us, to take root in us, to change us through and through. If we find the resilience to make peace with the unknown, to not require every answer to keep moving forward, to believe that everything will work out one way or another—we begin to live more completely in the moment, releasing the illusions that had been clouding us all along.

DAY 51

It may seem as though other people stumble upon their dream lives, but the truth is that everything inspiring is layered upon itself through time. Everything is continuously and consciously chosen, over and over again, until it forms into reality. Soulmate relationships are built. Dream careers are built. Resilient people are built—often with the pieces of their own greatest failures, mistakes, and missteps. You do not have to be perfect. You just have to keep going. *You have to keep moving in the direction of your dreams.*

11/07/20

DAY 52

Not everything you lose is a loss. Some things are a freedom. Some things are a second chance. Some things are a miracle in disguise. Some things are a detachment long-needed, a clarity brought to blurry eyes. Some things are an intervention. Some things are the unexpected answer to a long-chanted prayer. Some things are a healing. Some things are a becoming. Some things are planned long before you ever came to be. Some things are a devastation, but others are a kind of vital guidance, the kind of course-correction you did not even know you needed. The kind you did not even realize you were asking for all along.

12071202)

D A Y   5 3

Nothing is wrong with you. You are supposed to have days in which you are so self-assured followed by nights where you gaze into the sky and wonder if this is all there is. You are supposed to have years that feel like weeks and weeks that feel like years. You are supposed to get rejected sometimes. You are supposed to have people disagree with you at times. You are supposed to be a little lost now and again. You are not supposed to have all of the answers. *Nothing is wrong with you.*

DAY 54

You will not truly feel settled until you have done what you came here to do. Until you have reached into yourself and pulled out the most glimmering thing about you, and held it up for the world to see. Until you have completed the work that only you could do, in only the way that you can do it. Until you have made your gifts into an offering. Until you have stopped trying to live up to some ancient concept of perfection, but instead seek the radiating fullness of a life devoted to that which you alone are most suited for, what you alone are most destined to complete.

14/07/2020

DAY 55

Life is a blank canvas upon which our subconscious minds paint pieces of our souls. What matters is not so much what's in front of you, but what's within it that you see. That is what will tell you everything you need to know.

15|07|2025

DAY 56

You're not looking for anyone else to give you the answers, you're looking for what you already know to be reflected back to you. You already know what's true.

DAY 57

If you have a heart that is healing, what you need to remember is that there is more to life than romantic love. There are equal joys. There are other worthwhile pursuits. Even if romantic love is an element of your life, it is not the only thing life is about. It might be that the fabric of our society hinges on you believing that matrimony and reproduction are the end-all-be-all, the highest-high, the only thing truly worth living for. It may be well-intentioned people who do not want you to experience what they themselves fear. But romantic love does not excuse you from the inner work. It does not solve your every problem, and often, a rush to find it complicates our hearts the most. The pressure to be in a relationship creates a complex that can bend your sense of self until connection feels futile. Love exists in myriad ways, but the assumption that this singular form of it will lift you up above your human experience, sanitize your pain, and make the rest of your days a fever dream is not only untrue, it's unhelpful. It is placing the portal to your own inner peace within the realm of someone else's commitment rather than leading you back to where it truly exists: in your own ability to retrain your mind to perceive love at any given moment. Our fantasies about other people are never really about how someone else might give us their love. Instead, they mirror our unawakened love back to us. They serve to show us not that we need to seek another human heart but that we need to remember to nurture the one we already have.

DAY 58

Throughout your day, you may have thoughts that try to steer you off your path. They might be intrusive, sudden, and consuming. Their intensity and frequency will differ at times, but they can always exist in some form. Your job is to notice them before they convince you that they are true, that they are some kind of compelling guidance. You must learn to ask yourself: *Where does this thought intend to bring me?* Is it attempting to give a deeper clarity, or disturb calmed waters? It is something my most empathetic, compassionate, empowered self would believe? Must I choose to act on it? Will I?

DAY 59

The measure of a life well-lived is not how often you have avoided discomfort, pressure, or change, but the grace with which you navigated it. To say that you faced not even a fraction of resistance within your life proves nothing more than that you were defined by nothing: tried for nothing, stood for nothing, did nothing with the gifts that were given to you. I know it seems like the absolute worst thing in the world is to be disapproved of, but the actual worst thing is to paralyze yourself under the guise that you might be able to avoid any friction. The merit is not in whether or not you have ever experienced anything challenging, but the courage with which you faced what challenged you. That is what matters. That is what defines who you are.

DAY 60

When you feel a connection waning, that is when you must remind yourself not to steer another human being's destiny. That is when you must remind yourself that you cannot assume the dream you had for them is the same one they have for themselves. To love someone is to allow them to be sovereign. It is to honor their path and their ability to choose how they want to spend their time and their life. Learning to love in this way is the only way to experience true intimacy, not formed upon the basis of expectation or need, but the free will of two souls who see no more preferable way to spend their energy than on one another. That is what you are really waiting for—love that is intuitive and clear, that does not make you question or doubt how worthy you are of being prioritized, of being invested in. Love that chooses you as you choose it.

DAY 61

Rather than spending more of your time trying to work through your conceptual self, move out of your head and touch your life. Do just one thing differently than you did before. Care for yourself in the quietest, most intimate ways. Your idea of yourself will reform as you give yourself solid, undeniable, consistent proof that you are different than you once believed yourself to be.

2107 1200

DAY 62

Losing yourself is not always a bad thing. The point is to lose some versions of yourself. The point is to let some parts of yourself disintegrate within the fire of your personal transformation. You are meant to grow as new evidence and experience are presented to you, as you adapt to new ideas, solve new problems, gain new skills, hear new perspectives, and see more of the world as it really is. You are not meant to remain one static character within your life. When someone says to you, *you've changed,* you should reply, *how have you not?*

DAY 63

Not everyone is going to understand your journey because not everyone is meant to. Not everyone has made peace with their inner longings, nor paused to sincerely reflect upon themselves, or how they really intend to be. The nature of your transit will only emphasize some people's stuckness, the fortress around themselves that they've come to feel is an essential shield they cannot live without. What can be so unnerving about someone else's development is the part of ourselves we recognize as desiring that same change so deeply—and what it is within us that resists it in equal measure. Please remember that your experience is not validated in proportion to how much sense it makes to others. Even if you are the only person in the entire world who knows where you are going, that is more than enough to make it all the way there.

DAY 64

Maybe this phase of your journey is supposed to be about preparation. Maybe it's about developing the courage to take those first steps. Maybe it's about finding the stamina to keep going even when you're challenged, even when you become discouraged, even on the days you feel exhausted and it seems as though you'll never arrive. Maybe this part of your journey is about observing—studying the world you want to be a part of, the experiences you want to have, the person you want to be. Maybe you aren't supposed to be there yet. Maybe there are still dreams inside of you that have not yet come to light.

DAY 65

When you know who you are becoming, it is a lot easier to make peace with who you've been. It's a lot easier to dissect the past for the lessons you needed to learn, and then let the rest go. The experiences that delivered you those essential pieces of knowledge—no matter how uncomfortable they were at the onset—were not useless. They were not wasted. Your pain was not for nothing, your hurt was not meaningless. You completed the most daring task of all, which is to look into the recesses of your own fear and find hope, find meaning, and find a greater truth.

DAY 66

The fire can only burn what is not meant to be.

26/07/2021

DAY 67

Your story is not for everyone. If they have not proven that they intend to hear you and hold you gently, you are under no obligation to share the most raw details of yourself with them. There are some things you are allowed to keep sacred, that you are allowed to keep small. This is not denying yourself, it is protecting yourself. It is reminding yourself that in a world where it has become normal to broadcast every detail of your existence, it is okay to practice discernment. It is okay to be intentional about who holds your most vulnerable pieces.

27/07/2025

DAY 68

Nobody is brave at the beginning. Bravery is dug out of the deepest part of us, often by necessity. It is when you allow your love for something to grow a little larger than your fear about it. It is when you make the voice of possibility a little louder than the one of doubt. It is when you feel that familiar sense of hesitation come over you and choose to act anyway, when you decide to keep moving in the right direction even if you have to do it one step at a time. It is that moment of clarity when you realize that nobody—not one of us—gets to the end of this life with our hearts entirely unscarred, because that would mean they were also untouched. You become brave when you realize that wholeness allows for the nuances of who you are. You become brave when you realize that you do not have to always feel calm and certain, but be able to find the strength to keep showing up regardless.

DAY 69

You are not the ways in which you had to harden yourself to get through the chapters you had no other way to face. You are not the person you became to cope with the experiences you would never have chosen for yourself. You are the person who is confronting these empty parts of yourself and releasing them. You are the person who is asking yourself to keep going, who is asking to keep healing. You are the person who is still here today.

25/07/2021

DAY 70

There is nothing scarier than the idea of leaving what is good for the hope of what may be exceptional. What you do not realize, at that moment, is that you have already decided. The path forward is now about becoming comfortable with that choice, through all the mental gymnastics, justifications, explanations, and processing that it may bring. In the end, you already know. You are not finding your answers. You are finding your courage.

DAY 71

All of those little incongruences, the hiccups in the timing, the things that slipped right through your fingers and fell away—they are not always the result of a chaotic universe screwing up, but an intelligent one stepping in. Trust in the way the microcosms sometimes falter, as there are far more important things being constructed in their wake.

DAY 72

If you feel like you need to be where you are for a little while longer, you are probably right. If you feel like there's more to release, there probably is. If you think you're on the precipice of the breakthrough, you probably are. Just because you can't see the end yet, or understand how it will all come together, does not mean that you aren't still exactly where you are meant to be.

01/08/2024

DAY 73

Not every moment of every day can contribute to a perfect sequence of life experiences, but you will find purpose in the most subtle moments. Even the most senseless series of choices and coincidences will bring you somewhere profoundly clear; it's impossible to know the full impact of the moment you are in right now. You don't have to trust in what you cannot yet see, but be willing to give yourself wholly to this moment and let it transform you in the ways it's trying to. You know more than you think you do.

DAY 74

Sometimes, the walls that you once constructed as a safe-guard become the same thing that prevents your love from pouring into your own life. The thing that prevents your heart from knowing the inside of someone else's. What once kept you safe begins to hold you back—the series of self-defeating ideas that serve little purpose other than to dissuade you from connection, than to remind you not to reach out from behind your fortress, lest you get burned. Lest you get hurt. Sometimes, the only way to break down those walls is piece by piece. You have to let yourself be seen in the smallest ways. Then you have to keep going, and keep growing. You don't have to wake up tomorrow and be instantly better. You just have to practice thawing out what's gone cold and stiff within you. Do not allow your comfort zone to become your cage.

DAY 75

Nobody tells you that death and rebirth can occur all in the same body. That the past, once so familiar, can begin to feel like a fact that can be recalled but holds within it no attachment, as every cord to it has been released. Nobody tells you that the experiences once so clear within your mind can fade into nonexistence; nobody tells you that you will eventually think about every last thing that haunts you for the very last time, and you will not even realize it is the last. Nobody tells you that there are parts of you that you will come to meet that feel like new beings emerging from nothingness, right alongside the pieces of you placed down years ago that you assumed you'd never find again. Nobody tells you that some things will always remain. Nobody can explain the intricacies and complexities of what your life will be about, because that is for you and you alone to determine. That is the revelation that you alone are meant to experience—the part where every dead end weaves together into a storyline more beautiful than you could ever consciously write. This is what it means to be fully alive—not to always know where you are headed, but to know that eventually, you will arrive.

04|08|202)

DAY 76

If another person's love does not make you feel safe enough
to open up, if it does not make you see yourself more kindly,
if it does not make you want to live more in the ways you'd
always intended—it is not for you. Not because you are not
deserving, but because you are actually completely deserving
of someone who makes you feel happiness not only when
you are with them, but also when you are not.

05108(202)

DAY 77

There's something about learning to live with a positive curiosity—to course-correct the constant wondering of what may be going wrong, what is hinging on collapse, what grave error or misstep you have not accounted for. Turn your capacity to downboard-think into something that supports your growth. Consider, instead, how you might be pleasantly surprised, how it may be easier than you think, that there might be some vital lesson or realization attempting to emerge through your current experience. Consider, instead, how infrequently the worst case scenario has ever come to pass, and then consider how ruminating on it isn't protecting you from it, but allowing your mind to piece and filter that particular reality more clearly into form.

DAY 78

If you understand that life is about the little things, you will never find yourself wanting more than what's in front of you. You will understand that true joy is using what you have, being where you are, and loving the souls who have chosen to walk with you. You will begin to understand that the desire for grandiosity is a projection of the lack of true depth you feel within.

DAY 79

You don't have to run forever. The answers you're looking for have probably been with you all along. The journey is about strengthening your inner resolve to choose what you have always known is right, even if the world would not understand, even if you might disappoint some people, even if it might scare you or challenge you or make you feel vulnerable in a way you never have before. I hope you will discover that making it is not always about where you end up, but how you take each step. When you change your relationship with today, you change your relationship with tomorrow.

DAY 80

No, you will not be able to avoid hurting, but you will get better at it with time. You will learn to hear someone's disapproval and not immediately internalize it but simply witness it as their experience: one that does not have to touch you, nor sway or force you to react. You will feel your nervous system activate and your heart pound, and you will not self-destruct as though that may act as a Band-Aid, as though it could soothe you in some masochistic way. You will sense when you are tired and burnt out, and you will decide to love yourself enough to resist the urge to keep engaging and simply rest. You will learn about yourself enough to know when you need quiet, when you need connection, and when you need nurturing in the most basic ways—and you will learn how to give that to yourself. You will be rejected, and it will not end you; it will not initiate your own internal collapse. No, you will not be able to avoid hurting altogether, but you will become better able to weather it in time.

DAY 81

You live in a world that tells you to work in eight hour stretches, and that is productivity. You live in a world that tells you to devote forty years of your life to a career you are lukewarm about, and that is safety. You live in a world that tells you to surround yourself with as many people as possible, and that is connection. You live in a world that tells you to pack your schedule with as much as you can, and that is fullness. You live in a world that aims to slowly lose what it is that makes you feel most alive, and that is responsibility. Of course you feel disillusioned. Of course it hurts. We have built a society that does not often cater to the layers, intricacies, and changes that a human soul phases through. You will have to learn to create your own universe within that world—and maybe, just maybe, the waves you initiate for yourself will touch someone else, will inspire another person to move in the same way. Maybe your life will be a lighthouse for the other aching hearts yearning to know that there is another way to walk through their years, that there is still hope amid it all.

10/08/2020

D A Y 8 2

Some days the point is simply to be in the garden, to walk without a destination in mind. To write and never find the end of the sentence. To love without knowing entirely where that love will lead. To listen and not speak. To find salve in the quiet moments that nobody else will see. Maybe you are not meant to find an answer in every hour, but to finally realize that not everything is an open-ended question—some things are meant to just be.

11/08/2024

DAY 83

If it keeps bringing your attention back toward it, there is a lesson within it that still needs to be extracted. There is a piece you still need to pick up. There is an element you need to dissect, a wisdom you are meant to carry forth. You are not broken for not being able to effortlessly release. You are being asked to look at yourself with full honesty, and see an empty space in which you are actually primed for the most dramatic growth. It keeps calling to you because there's something it wants you to do with it, there's something within it that still wants to be seen.

DAY 84

It is heavy because you are not supposed to carry it this far, for this long. It is heavy because it was never really yours in the first place. It is heavy because humans are not meant to keep holding within them relics of the most painful parts of the past. It's heavy because it's carrying an old world into a new one. It's heavy because it's asking you to put it down. It's heavy because some part of you can sense who you would become without it. It's heavy because you've lightened in some way, and so the fragmented parts of you that are too dense to move with you must finally be put to rest.

DAY 85

Your authenticity is not your stream-of-consciousness. It is not doing whatever you want, whenever you want, without any regard or consideration for the ripple effect it might cause, for where it may lead. What you do consistently comes to be characteristic of you. Not what you think, feel or even fear, but what you choose. If you display sincere kindness even if you feel the hardness of judgment first wash over your awareness, you will come to be known as kind. If you display resiliency, strength, and courage even when you are facing the deepest unknowns, resilience will come to be associated with you, too. You are in some ways fixed, but in others, adaptable, mendable, and shiftable. You are not the culmination of what you once were. You can defy the past. You can become what you decide to be.

14|08|2020

DAY 86

Happiness is something that is gently built. It is what you make ritual within your life, what you allow yourself to get used to. You think of happiness as a constant forward motion, a kind of growing that looks like a never-ending accumulation, when it is in truth consistent effort in the same direction. It is the way you strengthen bonds, uncover beauty, and grow to become most comfortable with yourself. It is how you learn to trace the lines of your innermost desires outward into the world, to find within them the pockets where you most belong. It is to live in a way that makes you feel grateful you are here, that affirms how connected you are to something greater, that makes you feel as though you're working toward something that one day will add up to be more meaningful than all its parts.

DAY 87

Instead of trying to figure out whether or not something is definitely right for you, just notice what creates resonance or dissonance. Ask yourself if it makes your body gently contract or expand. Ask yourself if it gives at least as much energy as it takes. Ask yourself if it intrigues you, fascinates you, compels you. Ask what is there to be found. Ask where walking this path might lead. Pay attention to your body's most subtle responses: the way you lightly open or close yourself to the experience, and tally up the smallest coincidences. Let yourself be guided in the quietest ways.

D A Y   8 8

A big part of finding yourself is discovering the pieces of yourself you first see in other people. The other human beings who embody something so familiar but seemingly out of reach, who can evoke within you the heaviness of envy or the lightness of inspiration—both equally attempting to guide you to self-realization. Please, whatever you do, never forget that what you observe in others is also dormant in you. You are not coming into knowledge of a space in which you lack but a space in which you are most primed to expand and grow. The tension is not the result of another person occupying what could be yours to stand in, but the revelation of how much you are suppressing that they allow to flow out of themselves—how much they are willing to embrace. Your ego will want to make people like this your enemies. Your soul knows that they are your teachers in disguise.

DAY 89

Not giving up on yourself—not giving into your worst impulses—doesn't always look like winning an invisible war, but rather, putting your hands up and finally asking yourself, *what do I need to change here?* It's finally surrendering to the strength within that has been trying to tell you that you're off track. It's finally learning to work with yourself, to follow your own guidance. To listen, to hear, to respond. To love yourself in the most basic ways. To understand that your lack of constant momentum is not a defect within you, but a guide so strong, even your strongest attempts cannot overpower its wisdom. It is coming into the knowing that there is something within the quiet that needs to be heard.

DAY 90

It is easy to see all that is wrong within the world, but harder to dive inward—the place from which all the world is born. It is easy to know that something must be amended, but harder to actually make the amendment within our own perception first. It is easy to know where there is a lack of love, but harder to reach down within ourselves and let it come from us first. It is easy to realize what must change, but harder to be the one that changes it.

DAY 91

What if you knew that you were never meant to get it right the first time, but to build it through trial and error? How much more grace would you give yourself, how much more human might you be? How much more could you gain from your experiences if your expectation wasn't that you were supposed to be initially and unquestionably perfect, but that the sculpting of your soul would emerge through the consistency by which you showed up and kept trying, kept going, kept forging yourself through the fire of your own fear?

20\08\2024

DAY 92

Enough is not a point you reach but a feeling in your heart. A contentment, a knowing that you are where you're supposed to be. Nobody else can give that to you. Nobody else can hand you self-acceptance or inner belonging. Sometimes, our focus on other people's perceptions of us is a way to supplant our sense that something isn't quite right, as if by convincing those around us that we are on our true path, we might somehow be a little closer than we were before. We cannot trick our hearts with our minds. We cannot list off the facts that quantify and outline our enoughness. We can only come to the quiet, little place inside us and honor that. We can only exit the labyrinth of our own pain when we realize that self-love is not an outward measure but an inward nurturing.

21|08|2021

DAY 93

Your experience of today is constructed from the minor choices of yesterday. Where you left your shoes, the email you didn't answer, and the appointment you forgot you made. The lingering emotions wandering through your insides undigested, unplaced. The more you get better at anticipating your future needs, the easier it becomes to be present within your life. The more you learn to live in this equilibrium, you find it easier and easier to sip the tea and not worry about so many other things, because they're settled. Even if they're not, you trust yourself to handle them. You do not need to reactivate your nervous system and pump yourself full of adrenaline-fueled focus to remember to take care of what needs caring for. Your choices must begin to reflect not just the person you are, but also the one you are becoming.

DAY 94

Listen to the parts of you that are trying to be heard. The parts of you that speak softly, that gently show you where you are not open, where you are still stuck, where you are asking to grow, and who you are asking to love. Sometimes, our dominant stream of thinking is not the most clear representation of our truest inner selves. Our bodies speak in subtle ways, and as we learn to pay attention to not only what we hear, but also what we sense, we awaken an entirely new level of living, an entirely new way of being.

23|08|2022

DAY 95

You either see things through a critical lens, or a creative one. You either spend your life constantly evaluating how each thing around you is not enough, or you shift your perspective to wonder how you can turn all that you have into anything you ever wanted. You either seek out and focus on the ways in which you are imperfect, or you see within those imperfections cracks through which your greatest growth, your greatest purpose, and your greatest vision will emerge.

DAY 96

Maturity is realizing that you are not supposed to be for everyone. You are not the center of everyone's universe. At the same time, you are the creator of your own. You get to decide who gets to be a part of your story, and how much. You get to play with the forces of inspiration that come through you, or you get to let them pass you by. You get to decide what is for you, rather than just trying to fit yourself into the sidelines of a life centered on someone else.

25|08|202)

DAY 97

Your inner wisdom isn't supposed to give you every answer to your entire life, but to show you to the next right step. You are not supposed to be able to intuit every turn the road may take, because that would defeat the entire purpose of being here; that would defeat the entire purpose of being alive. Nobody—not one of us—knows everything that might unfold. Our job is not to get better at predicting, projecting, or becoming attached to uncertain possibilities, but having sincere faith that what we know needs to happen next is the key that eventually unlocks everything we've been waiting for, everything we've ever wanted to be.

DAY 98

When you love your life exactly the
way it is, it transforms into everything
you've always wanted it to be.

DAY 99

Heavy feelings are not asking for your intervention, they are asking for your attention. When you come into full awareness of what you feel, the feeling will gradually release itself. You participate in your suffering when you take action to delay, avoid, resist, or fracture that awareness of your feeling states and end up stuck beneath them. You will probably feel really reactive when you start to pay attention to the sensations going on inside your body. When you begin to come into awareness of each one that makes you uncomfortable, you're going to want to jump to fix, change or do something that could make the feeling go away. It doesn't, though, because the feeling isn't in the things you're fixing, changing, or distracting yourself with. The feeling is in you. It is not asking to be put onto some physical form within the world, but simply to be metabolized, processed, and eventually churned into an unconscious wisdom that will guide you forward in ways more powerful than you can even perceive from where you currently stand.

DAY 100

Life knows things you don't. It's heard conversations you haven't. It's realized the truth about some people you have not yet completely come to know. Trust life when it seems like the very things you want most suddenly no longer want you back. You have to believe that life is protecting your heart from any further damage. It is ensuring you will not waste another hour of your precious time on what's not in your best interest. Life is not turning its back on you, so you must learn to not turn your back on it.

25|08|202)

DAY 101

It is okay to want a quiet kind of life. A life that is biggest within the little things, the moments that are not so overt in their impressiveness, but if you really pay attention, open up a space in your chest most people have not yet realized even exists. It is okay to want an easy kind of life. A life that is filled not so much with reaching, but simply placing your hand down on all that is in front of you right now. A life where you move at your own pace, create in your own time. A life where you hope your legacy will be one of a constant, loving presence. Where you reminded others of how much goodness can exist within a human soul.

DAY 102

You are meant to change. You are meant to change your mind. You are meant to change your perception. You are meant to change what you think you want within this world. You are meant to evolve, you are meant to adapt, you are meant to grow. You are meant to shed old layers. You are meant to let go. The body is designed to digest and metabolize and renew itself, cell by cell, and thought by thought. Trust the process. Realize that we don't ever really have to let go; we just have to accept what's already gone. We don't have to grieve what we think the world took, but to remember that whatever beauty we grew within our lives is still within us—and wherever we go, and whatever we do next, we will grow it there, too. Everything that's truly meant for you will be waiting for you on the other side, because everything that's truly meant for you is still within you. It always has been.

DAY 103

The truth is that it has to challenge you in order to change you. It has to make you question whether the parameters you live within are truly your limits or simply the edge of what you've grown comfortable with. The truth is that it has to stop you in order to redirect you. It has to test you before it can reward you; it has to trust you before it can open the floodgates. The truth is that it has to bring you to your knees before it can lift you back up into an entirely new reality. It has to show you what's wrong for you before you'll understand what's right.

DAY 104

You don't need a life without a fight.
You need a life worth fighting for.

DAY 105

If you spend your days trying to make every piece of the picture fit prematurely, you're going to miss out on what the journey was really supposed to be about—simply being in it. Allowing all of the mismatched elements of who you are to coexist, come together, or fade apart when it's time. Loving some, losing others, and noticing who stays. Realizing that there are a thousand forms of love that ask to come to you. Letting your inner guidance lead you to a story far more beautiful than you could write on your own. *You don't have to know the ending to be perfectly on path.* You don't have to understand right now. Peace awaits in the acceptance of the things you were never supposed to change.

DAY 106

It takes strength to witness your own patterns and correct your course. It takes strength to resist what's become so familiar. Most people will never realize how deeply the compulsion to repeat can run, how entrenched we can become in the paths we've walked over and over again, until we cannot see anything beyond them. It takes strength to choose differently, to believe in what you can sense but not yet see. It takes strength to be different, to be humble, and to change. It takes strength to become the person you've always wanted to be.

DAY 107

Resilience isn't always toughness. Sometimes, it's the softness to simply let things move through you. Sometimes, it's the willingness to not act on emotions you would not want more fully expressed, but just to feel them and let them go.

DAY 108

It is painful to end your suffering. It is painful to process, to feel, to let go. It is painful to grieve, to be honest, to move on. It is so painful that most people keep themselves in a prolonged state of mild discomfort so as to avoid the acute but temporary sensation of facing their fears. It is painful to end your suffering at first—but then there is peace on the other side. There is a new life waiting to begin.

06/09/2024

DAY 109

The very nature of your hurting is actually a sign that something within you is still fighting. Still fighting for peace. Still hoping for something beautiful. Still knowing that there is so much more to you that you have yet to experience. Despite all it has been through, your heart is still asking you to let it be seen, to let it be loved. Something within you cares enough to shed all the layers of all the people you never really wanted to be. See, healing is a hard thing. It requires you to live in a way where you are no longer numbing yourself. To experience a high, you have to also embrace the low. Not because one necessitates the other, but because life is an unpredictable, unmistakable, gorgeous mess, and if you start showing up for it, you'll realize that the mark of a life well lived, a soul most loved, is not a person who is permanently composed. It is a person who can move all the experiences they desire without scaring themselves into the corner of just one.

07/05/2020

DAY 110

There is not one other human being alive who can accurately assess whether or not you are where you are supposed to be. Even if you have every external success in the world but know, deep inside, you are not fully fulfilled, then you have to trust that. You have to understand that your existence will not be evaluated by whether or not other people were impressed, but by whether or not your courage left an impression, an indelible mark, on the very nature of your being. Whether or not you brought yourself fully into this experience, and what you took away from it.

DAY 111

It is okay to disappear for a while to work on yourself. It is okay to disappear for a while and start over. It is okay to wipe the slate clean and begin again. The world as it is today does not give us the grace for the normal transitions you are meant to go through. You need to create space within your life to signify your internal growth, to mark for yourself the end of one chapter and the beginning of another.

DAY 112

If your worth is not self-evident to them, they are not worthy of your effort to convince them otherwise. A person who does not value you is not a challenge to see how much you can bend yourself to fit the mold of their preferences, how deeply you can lose yourself in their ideals, how quickly you can get them to change their mind. A person who does not value you does not see in you what you see in them, and that is not because they are a once-in-a-lifetime kind of person whose magic will not be recreated. They are a mortal being who you have graced with divine perception. When you turn your gaze to the next person who lights up your heart in that same way, you will see in them all the same. The light is in you. It always has been.

10|05|2024

DAY 113

When you're tired, rest. When you're motivated, act. When you're inspired, create. When you're hopeful, leap. When you're doubtful, wait. When you're ready, go. Those feeling states act as portals of possibility, and when you let them slide by, you choose not to enter the parallel reality it was pulling you toward. Listen to your body, and listen to your soul. These emotions are rarely random, but instead open and close doors at just the right time.

DAY 114

It is okay to say, *that is not for me*. It is okay to say, *I do not prioritize that right now*. It is okay to say, *that is not the experience I am looking for next*. Sometimes, it feels easier to draw deeper lines, to say something is just an impossibility when it is simply a misalignment. It takes time to stop conflating what you don't want with what you can't do. You cannot hold it all, not all of the time. Eventually, something has to give, something has to release. Instead of dizzying yourself with all the reasons you are incapable, consider your energy your most valuable investment, and share it accordingly.

DAY 115

Comfort becomes a vice when what once held you together begins to hold you back, when what's comfortable in the short-term makes you lose sight of what's best for you in the long-term. Comfort becomes a vice when nurturing yourself is only reaching for the most soothing thing you can find without asking what is dysregulating you in the first place. Comfort becomes a vice when what's familiar becomes the only thing that feels possible. Comfort becomes a vice when it does not help you face your fears, but run from them forever.

DAY 116

When you think that if you finally let yourself run free, you will inevitably fall down, what you usually don't realize is that you're already on the ground. Staying where you are is a perceived safety—this life was not given to you to be just endured, but experienced. This life was not given to you to die before you're dead. This life was not given to you to arrive at the end in perfect condition. You may feel as though the worst possible scenario is that you fail, but it is, in fact, that your fear of failure paralyzes you from doing anything meaningful with the limited time you have.

DAY 117

The most loving things about you are what will survive you long after you are gone. Anything else is a shadow cast across your shimmering soul, here to teach you by contrast who you really are, and how you really are.

DAY 118

When you feel even the smallest bit of happiness, slow down. Stretch that moment as wide as you possibly can. Let it lead you to a space where everything seems possible, where anything could be. Allow it to invoke gratitude, and pay attention as you feel so at home, so at ease, so correct in your peacefulness. This is who you really are, although the storms may make you think otherwise. This is what you will always return to, no matter how many times you abandon yourself. This ever-present part of you is your true self, your whole self.

DAY 119

We don't move on when we think it's time. We move on when we slowly allow something a little more interesting, a little more beautiful, a little more compelling, to grab our attention, and move us into a new world of our own creation.

DAY 120

Your attention has an eclipsing effect on your life; what you pour your energy into becomes your energetic state. When you feel most stuck, it is because you have unknowingly cornered yourself with your consistent focus. The way out is to disengage, even just for a moment. Offer yourself to something, anything else. It does not need to be good, it does not need to be hopeful. It just needs to be different, it just needs to capture you, it just needs to pull you, it just needs to move you out of where you are and into somewhere new. It just needs to remind you that where you currently are is not the only place you can ever be.

18|05|202)

DAY 121

How do you know you're self-sabotaging? The storm isn't running out of rain because you're chasing the clouds. You're seeking them out because you think you don't deserve the light of day. There are things we all endure, but not always. The night does not go on forever, but our minds can make us think this is so. The storm can become our comfort zone. It can turn into the one space where we feel free enough to actually take care of ourselves, to actually say no to the world, to actually find ourselves, to actually choose what's true to us, to actually express the feelings that we otherwise bottle up and hide. Your journey is not about how fast you outrun the rain, but whether or not you stop and ask yourself what part of you feels nourished by it, and if there is a better way.

19|05|2020

DAY 122

Sometimes, things don't unfold on your timeline because they are occurring on one that is far greater. Sometimes, the things you'd choose for yourself only rise to the level of your broken self-perception. Sometimes, when the light hits your eyes after staring for so long into the darkness, it is painful. Sometimes, life is trying to give you more than you'd ever take for yourself, and you should let it. You should let it lead you higher than you'd ever expect to go.

DAY 123

What matters is that, in the end, you can tell a story that you're proud of. That's the light to hold all of your decisions up to: *when you're old and retelling the stories of your life, what will you say?*

21|05|2021

DAY 124

Every human being you know, everyone you walk past
on the street, everyone you judge, everyone you think you
dislike, everyone that you think is nothing like you—they
are also fighting a quiet battle inside them. There is a hurt
inside of them that feels quite a lot like your own. The faces
of our demons may differ; we may call them various names,
and we may feel their presence more at some times than
others, but, at the end of the day, they all haunt us in similar
ways. This is what it really means to come into deep awareness of what it means to be human—to understand that we
all live with an internal longing of some kind. Have compassion because no matter how it appears on the surface,
every person, including you, has a mountain all their own.

22|05|202J

DAY 125

Not every piece of you is malleable.
Not every element of you wants to
be fixed, or needs to be.
There are some that simply ask to be loved.

DAY 126

Figuring other people out isn't as hard as it might seem. People are so much more direct and transparent than the stories we wind around them. The way they are behaving is the way they feel—and people contain complexities. They're acting hot and cold because they are confused. They're making time for what they really value, they're showing up for what feels comfortable and aligned. They may still care, but if they tell you, *not now*, they mean it. If they tell you, *not me*, they mean it. If they tell you, *you deserve more*, they mean it. But they also mean it when they say they love you and show you that they do. They mean it when they stay to weather your toughest storms together, and when they show you respect. They mean it when they look at you with love. Take away all of the words a person has ever spoken to you, and observe what they do. That is how they feel, and that is who they are. Your choice is how much of them you want in your life.

DAY 127

Arriving is not, *I can have anything I want.*
It is, *I already have everything I need.*

25/09/2022

DAY 128

Once you introduce a new thread into the fabric of your reality, it is all different. It has all changed. Instead of thinking you have to reinvent yourself all at once, shift one, tiny aspect of your existence, and watch as the simple act of that victory becomes a wave of transformation that will pierce through your life as a whole.

26|05|2024

DAY 129

Growing up is realizing it's not all for you. Not every trend, not every moment, not every person, not every opportunity, not every idea. It's not all going to fit, it's not all going to flow, it's not all going to apply. But it's also learning to not see this as a negative. It's learning to become the best version of yourself, not somebody else.

DAY 130

Placing down what you carry isn't just putting it down, it's unpacking it piece by piece. It's holding it up and asking *is this mine, is this true?* This is what it means to find yourself, and to heal. This is what it means to truly move on. To take the things that you cannot loosen your grip on and ask why you are so tightly wound around them. To discover what they are meant to show you, to alchemize them into catalysts for change.

DAY 131

To clear your psychic weight, you must draw lines from one chapter to the next, end one version of yourself and welcome the next. You do not have to ruminate on what you once did because you are not that person anymore. You are different, and so is your life. With time, those memories will fade into a distant recollection, and most will disappear forever. You are allowed to close the door. You are allowed to let go. You are allowed to find your new, solid ground in the knowledge that you have learned the lessons you needed to, and you will walk forward with more grace, more self-awareness, and more patience. You will become who you always needed to be.

DAY 132

Please do not allow the heaviness of what holds you to dissuade you from believing in the vision that calls you. Please do not assume that your fear is a finality, a sign of impossibility. Please do not think that just because it is hard, or will take time, or feels far off right now, that you will not one day arrive. One day, everything you fear will never come will be right in front of your eyes.

DAY 133

The capacity to enter deep and complex feeling states is a sign of your inner strength and ability to process a more nuanced experience of being human. When you are more sensitized to one aspect of your experience, the rest becomes more vivid as well. It takes a lot of courage not to numb yourself out, or distract yourself through your hours and days. It takes a lot of heart to be willing to hurt, to be willing to open up, to be willing to keep trying, no matter how many times you must keep rediscovering your inner flame.

DAY 134

May this be the year you learn to believe in yourself. May this be the year you find the strength to change what you cannot accept. May this be the year that you start to see things differently, that you begin to let go. May this be the year you're guided to the souls who will see you, who will love you as you are. May this be the year you look back upon and realize you have lived an entire lifetime within it, that the person you were at the beginning is not the person you find at the end. May this be the year you do not give up on who you were meant to be.

02/10/2002

DAY 135

You will laugh again. You will be in the moment again. You will love again. You will find yourself again. You will get into a routine again. You will believe in something bigger than yourself again. You will return because you're not going backwards, but softening inwards. You are bringing into expression the person who has always lived inside. You have not lost the hope within you, for it is the home that will always be your final destination, your ultimate truth realized.

01|10|2023

D A Y   1 3 6

That love you seek? It's already here. Open the
floodgates. Let what's living inside of you refract
around you and come pouring back in.

DAY 137

The structures of the world serve to provide a framework for the human experience, to instill a sense of order and principle. When you are young, you learn and live by them. Then, if you are lucky, they are disrupted by some newfound sense of awareness. They become unraveled by your consciousness, and whether you realize it or not, you graduate to the next level of experience, one where you are able to hold space for contrast, for difference, for complexity and nuance. One where you are able to grow, to deepen, and to become more present. Arriving isn't a matter of completing, it's a matter of knowing it's already done.

DAY 138

One day, you will wake up and realize that the pieces all came together faster than you thought, and in a way you never would have imagined. You will see the purpose in the lessons, in the pacing, in what left and what stayed. You will see that you've carried everything you've ever learned with you, that all that wisdom is still inside. Most of all, you will see that it's still imperfect, and always will be. Arriving isn't a matter of completing, as that would be the end. Arriving is a matter of trusting it's all going to be okay.

06110120U

DAY 139

If you see it, love it, and you know that it is not yet yours, study it. Examine it. Spend as much time with it as possible. Ask yourself: *what makes this beautiful to me?* This is how you get to know yourself, this is how you define your contours, your edges, the distinctions that make you who you really are. This is how you come to understand what it is you really want to create, what really inspires you, what really makes you want to be alive.

DAY 140

The voice of your inner limitation will cry loudly when you begin to surpass it. It will tell you that this new world is not safe, for it is unknown. It will enshroud you with visions of all that might fall apart, all that could go wrong. What it does not know is that you are a child of the universe, no different than the branches, rivers, and vines. The force animating all things also flows through you, and will support you, no matter which way you choose to go.

08110120L)

DAY 141

The development of self-worth is the practice of no longer denying yourself what you find to be beautiful. You see a piece of clothing you would love to wear and your heart instantly gives you a little warmth to say "yes." Then your mind interrupts your flow and says, *but not on you.* You see a place you'd love to live, and you envision all that might unfold there. Then your mind interrupts and says, *but not for you.* You imagine a creative project that would light you up on the inside, but your mind interrupts and says, *for a better artist.* If you enter a lovely, peace-filed hour, do not let your mind interject and remind you that such lovely, little things are not for you. In the quiet, allow yourself to experience what you once believed you didn't deserve.

DAY 142

Everything that seems effortless is almost always the result of effort so exceptional, it appears nonexistent. That is what inner growth is like. When you arrive, you appear entirely at peace, flowing gently through the days. What becomes invisible through this transit is the aching heart you had to hold as it healed, the pain you had to find meaning in, the ways in which you had to reconcile everything that didn't make sense and form a new worldview through it. Everything that seems effortless is almost always the result of the most extraordinary human feats.

DAY 143

When it comes to loving other people, they mostly just want to be heard; they ultimately need to feel seen. In the same way that when you witness what it is you feel, it seems to alchemize the feeling, you can offer that to other people when you witness them. They don't always need you to solve a problem or interject or have a well thought out response. Sometimes, all they really need is someone to sit quietly with them, to listen even when their words are messy and going in circles, unsure of what they're really trying to say. Sometimes, all anyone really needs is someone who sees.

DAY 144

It does not matter how far you have wandered from your true self, there is always a way back. You may have lost some time. You may have wasted some energy. You may have learned some lessons harder than you ever needed to. These are moments you never get back, but it doesn't matter. You're realizing now. *You're realizing before it is too late.*

12/10/2021

DAY 145

You either live at the edge of your
curiosity, or from the backseat of your
doubt. Neither are perfectly comfortable,
but one is far more worthwhile.

DAY 146

How do you keep going, even when you're ready to give up?
You realize that sometimes, your inability to force yourself
to engage with the things you intuitively know your soul
has evolved beyond is the greatest sign of growth itself. It
means that you really have learned the lessons you needed
to, that you really are ready for the next level, the next experience. Your subconscious mind is at work designing an
entirely new game for you to play. You'll have to stop being
surprised that the old rules no longer work, or no longer
apply. You are not failing because your soul is not letting you
go backwards, or stay exactly where you are. Sometimes, the
greatest sign of growth is prioritizing rest and wellness, saying no, feeling more deeply, and expressing it more loudly.
What can seem as though it is your unraveling is sometimes
your rebalancing.

DAY 147

Everything is yours for a time, and then it isn't. Everything is borrowed, and everything is temporary while you are here. Yet you approach your life as though you have forever to live it. You go about each day imagining that tomorrow—when things are less busy, the kids are a little older, you're through this one phase, and the problem at the tip of your mind has resolved itself—you will let yourself actually be present in the day you greet. The illusion is that you're always one step away from freedom. It's not one step further into the external, it's one step inward. One step closer to realizing that this is all there is and this is more than enough.

15/10/2021

DAY 148

Love introduces the highest possible frequency into the equation, and so when it is present, it is transformative. Like a door cracking to expose a stream of light into an otherwise dark room, once love is present, fear begins to dissolve. If you need change, you need love, because the love itself will change whatever needs to be softened, lightened, and realigned.

DAY 149

To see yourself lovingly does not mean glossing over your imperfections, the breaks within your being, the ways in which you need to mend yourself from the inside and grow. It means to believe that you are capable of doing that healing, that you are strong enough to keep going—not only to make it through another day or another week, but to leap in the direction of your desires. To know that you can trust your own steadiness, that you can endure your own storms, that you can carry yourself through all the rest of your life.

DAY 150

When our desires are not directly expressed, they tend to manifest in subconscious, maladaptive, insidious ways. What's within needs a way out, and when those desires arrive into willing hands, our minds are given a chance to find the healthiest way to fulfill those deepest needs.

DAY 151

It is the courage with which you are willing to identify your shortcomings and name your failures and attempt to rise beyond them that will define the edges of your heart and depth of your soul. It is not whether or not you have ever made a wrong turn, but whether or not you were willing to find your way back to the path.

DAY 152

If you could make a list of everything you've ever worried about—everything you thought you'd never get over, every answer you thought you'd never find, every fear you thought would be the end of you—you'd realize that every single one passed. Despite your doubt, and despite your disbelief, a way forward was made. As time goes on, you will begin to see the magic in the process. You will begin to understand why things had to unfold precisely the way they did. You will realize that if you did not have the exact experiences you had just as you had them, you would have missed out on the essential lessons, tools, and pieces of wisdom that built you into the person you are today—the person who will keep walking you forward. When you look back on the past, you can see the purpose in how everything came to be, regardless of the twists and turns that brought you there.

20/10/2020

DAY 153

No, it is not comfortable to make your own way within this world. Yes, it is simpler to follow the well-walked path, one that is certain and clear. But it is far less comfortable to live with that quiet knowing within you that you were meant for something more, that you're here for something important, something your whole life has been preparing you for, waiting for you to choose. When the moment comes, learn to live beyond the expectations you once had for yourself. Have faith. Believe in yourself before anyone else does, because it is the consistency with which you act on your visions that enables them to transform from ideas into realities the entire world can see.

21110|2020

DAY 154

To truly pivot in life is not to move from one external path to another but to stop navigating your course solely from the blueprint given to you over the years. It does not mean to turn in a new direction, but to first go inward, to learn how to hear your own moment-to-moment instructions. It is to learn how to trust yourself, how to listen. It is to lead your life with a deeper degree of integrity. It is not to reconstruct your identity with pieces of what the world may deem more acceptable but to deconstruct the notion that you must fit within a mold at all.

DAY 155

It is your duty to see the best within yourself, because those that are aware of their own love, who believe in their own selves—they move through life differently. They are kinder, and more whole. They are more forgiving and more accepting and more willing to learn, to empathize, and to find strength. Whatever goodness you believe the world is missing is probably equivalent to a level of love resting dormant within you. Uncover it. Set it free.

23\10\2021

DAY 156

Follow the vision that you find to be most meaningful and most worthwhile. Not the vision the world attempts to superimpose on your psyche with all the charms and emblems of a life-well-lived: a human being going through the motions with the expectation and assumption that joy will somehow find them along the way. Design your life to your own liking, your own standard, your own inner peace. Rather than basing your decisions on how things appear, base them on how they feel.

DAY 157

Everything that is meant for you is still waiting for you. Even if you have failed in the past, even if you feel so stuck you cannot imagine making it through one more day. Even if you messed up every shot you were given, if you don't believe in yourself, if you're afraid, if you aren't sure how things will work out, and even if nobody else would understand. You still contain within you the potential of all you ever wanted to be. It is never too late.

DAY 158

The portal into your future life is often subtle. It is the gentle intuition that there's a trip that needs to be taken, a place that needs to be seen, an experience that needs to be had, a person that's waiting for you on the other side. You feel lost when you've walked by too many of these doorways, but there will always be more. There will always be beautiful experiences waiting for you to choose them wholeheartedly.

DAY 159

The growth is in the response. The healing is in who you choose to become, regardless of what you've done or what's happened in the past. When you look for the lesson, you find the silver lining. When you learn the lesson, you discover the purpose of the valley before the peak. You begin to understand that life is not about what you accumulate or accomplish, but who you become in the process, how much you can be awake in the day before it passes, how much you can believe in the unseen miracles inside that are waiting on you to unleash them into the world.

27\10\2021

DAY 160

Purpose is not a single act, it is a way of moving through the world that ensures everything you touch is infused with a little more love than it was before. It is a way of being that gives you softer eyes, the ability to see a little more potential, a little more hope, a little more possibility than the rest. It is not any one thing you do, but a way you become. A person you choose to be.

28/10/2021

DAY 161

When you're presented with a new idea that defies your own limitations for yourself, I hope you will not fight to preserve those limitations. I hope you will not spend more of your energy outlining why you cannot, when you could spend it envisioning how you might. I hope you will learn to think beyond the parameters of what you've previously assumed is possible, I hope you will be able to tell life what the end goal could be, and I hope you will be able to listen as life shows you how to get there.

DAY 162

The person you really are is not the one who shows up on Friday. Not the person on your résumé. Not the person other people have made you up to be. You are the person who wakes up in the morning and carries yourself through the day. You are the person who cries with grief and loves with all the hope you have left in you. You are the person who dreams, who tries, who fails, and who returns. You are so much more than what you appear to be. You are so much more than what anyone just looking on the surface could see.

DAY 163

Your internal commentary is either going to block the blessings, or it's going to let them in. Change the way you think and speak about what it is that's coming to you, what it is you're receiving, and you'll see the brightness of things often depends on how closely you are paying attention. The miracle is still occurring, whether or not you realize it.

DAY 164

Sustained expansion outward requires consistent nourishment inward. Remember this when it feels as though you need more rest and reassurance than ever. It is most likely because you are also growing and expanding in unprecedented ways.

06/11/2021

DAY 165

There's pretty much just one guiding principle, one thing you need to know to get you through the rest of your life. Whatever you feel most strongly about is the next thing that needs to happen. Don't worry about how it will all add up, or to where exactly it will lead. Consistency is the tonic that transforms your life into a dream of your own design.

DAY 166

There is so much power in the quiet. In allowing yourself to build and blossom without any additional energy swaying you one way or another, without any other light taking your attention and making you turn away from where you need to stay focused. There is so much power in what you do not say, in what you choose to keep your own.

D A Y 1 6 7

When you work on becoming the person you want to be, the things that are meant to be yours find you. It is so common to gaze at life and identify everything you feel you are missing, everything you wish would come to be. Rarely do you ask yourself if you are yet the kind of person who could not only handle what you are asking for, but actually embrace it, savor it completely. What you are asking for is not a particular person, circumstance or thing, but a feeling state: a level of experience you have never touched before. This does not happen to you when something arrives, rather, something arrives when you have carved out that depth within first. Then world around you begins to mirror it back.

04111202

D A Y 1 6 8

Can you imagine what your days would look like if you stopped doing all of the things you think you need to do to be cool and started giving yourself completely to the things that make you feel the most alive, the most like yourself? I will tell you—you'll get a life that feels like it was built from the inside out: your own personal dream come true, as opposed to a life in which you feel like a stranger, disconnected but still moving through the motions, wondering why it does not fill your heart when it seems to initiate so much approval and praise. The funny truth is that no matter which way you decide to lead your life, there will be people who resonate with it and people who don't. The difference is that when your life comes from a place that's authentic, you begin to attract the people, places, and experiences you actually want—not the ones you think you're *supposed* to want.

DAY 169

Sometimes, the disruptions on the surface of your life are like ripples upon deep bodies of water, revealing the invisible gaps on the Earth beneath. Long ago, you put to rest a dream that still lives inside and won't let you fully merge with a life that is not aligned with it. At your core, you know there is more, even if you have not the slightest clue how you might come to find it. You cannot make it work because there is a little part of you deep down that doesn't want it to. There's a little part that is trying to move in a different direction. What can appear on the surface as repeated failure is often your most life-giving internal navigation system leading you to the most important experience of your life.

DAY 170

How do you finally stop worrying? You realize that the version of yourself that will be able to handle every situation that might arise in your life will be born in the precise moment that situation comes to be. No matter where your path might take you, or where you go, the version of yourself that you will need in those moments will emerge right as you need it and not a second before. You cannot call upon all of the parts of yourself to exist at once. Different versions of you are needed for various aspects of your life. Find peace in knowing that you are more than one thing, and within the layers of who you are—both visible and invisible—exists a strength that is equal to or more powerful than anything you may come to face.

07/11/2024

DAY 171

In stillness, you are met with the most undeniable truth. That is why so many of us busy and distract ourselves, and turning up the volume of the noise around us so that we don't have to acknowledge what we already know. When you can sense a resistance to slowing down, ask yourself what it is that you do not want to see. That realization is the one that will set you free.

DAY 172

If it feels wrong with your fullest conviction, don't do it. Even if it will disappoint some people. Even if it will interrupt the trajectory you thought you needed to be on. Even if it will scare you. Even if it will call into question everything you thought you knew before. If it feels wrong with your fullest conviction, don't do it, because one day, you will look back and realize that there is a difference between fear and intuition. One you can reason with, and the other stands firm. When you find that firmness within you, honor it. It is a guide from deep within, and far beyond.

DAY 173

There is not one thing that withholds you from your life as much as living in other people's heads. When you operate with the unconscious belief that to experience love is to earn it from others, you exist to construct an image of who you are rather than the reality of who you might be. You heal from this when you come to understand that you cannot truly control how you are seen, you can only project. You assume. What you imagine others see is more telling of your subconscious psychology than any external perception. Understanding this unlocks wisdom about who you want to be. Rather than trying to get other people to see you a certain way, ask yourself to *actually become that way* in real time. That is the difference between grazing the surface of life, and diving all the way in.

DAY 174

If you are consistent in offering yourself loving thoughts, you begin to form a sanctuary around yourself. You begin to become your own refuge. You start to build a belief system rooted in your own certainty. The world and its opinions become less and less convincing as your foundation is built independently of how you're perceived, consumed, and responded to. You begin to understand that your experience of yourself is a sovereign thing; it is not hinged on how much you can be affirmed or appreciated. In that, you begin to form a wall of armor around yourself—not one that does not let love in, but one that is discerning about what is true, what is worthwhile, and what is allowed to enter.

11/11/2020

DAY 175

Becoming yourself is soulwork. It is reaching into the deepest parts of yourself and bringing them into the light. It is asking yourself the hardest questions until you arrive at the truest answers. It is discarding some of the coping mechanisms that you no longer want to be a part of you, and being consistent with the ones you do. It is keeping your word, firstly to your self. It is learning to lean into your kindest, most beautiful parts. It is finding yourself, and building that self outward. It is taking your spirit and bringing it into form.

DAY 176

Yes, things can change, often faster than you realize and in better ways than you could ever imagine. You have to find the courage to be uncomfortable, to process, to face things. More importantly though, you have to come into the clarity that life can be dramatically different from one chapter to the next. You will have other chances to be as you've always wanted, experience what you've always wanted. Things really will change, whether you are confident in them or not. There are few other guarantees.

DAY 177

One of the characteristics of having a big destiny is that things don't work out for you right away. There are delays and unexpected times of quiet. The plans you had for your life are unraveled and you're asked to conceive of a new vision, one grander than you had the capacity to imagine in the first place. These rest periods are actually life's way of giving you an opportunity to work on yourself, to invest in who you want to be. To heal, to release. These times are not just to be tolerated or waited through, but used. They are quiet gifts that will lead you to the path you were really meant to be on.

DAY 178

How do you heal when you can't remove yourself from what's causing the pain? You learn boundaries. You learn that none of us can insulate ourselves fully from the ache of the world, from other broken hearts, from inevitable stress. You learn that the journey was never about that, anyway; it's only ever been about strengthening yourself from the inside out. Training your mind to be more conscious of what it entertains. To act not out of compulsion or obligation, but true choice—out of self-preservation, and self-love. You look inward at what pieces of yourself you see within those who bother you most deeply, and you work on healing those pieces. You get better at communicating what you need. You make the changes that need to occur within your own life, and then you notice what gently alleviates the tension. You notice that the situation hasn't lightened, but you have. You have changed what moment you meet.

DAY 179

Half the battle is coming to the place of really believing you deserve good things. It's learning to account for all of your virtues and strengths as often as you do your shortcomings. It's starting to see that you are worthy of feeling good just because you are a human being trying your best, because life was never limited to only be about stretching you past your previous comfort zones—but to teach you to make a home once you're there. You, more than anyone else, have to want the best for yourself. That is the start of it all.

D A Y   1 8 0

To be unwavering does not mean to be linear within your own life experiences, but to continually return to the things that make you feel most at ease, aligned, lit up with possibility. These things that seem to awaken you from the outside are really pieces of yourself being shown to you in real-time. The whole world is like a painting with ink dropped in nonsensical shapes without clear borders, flowing and merging in unpredictable ways. What matters is not what picture is being painted, but what within the image you see.

DAY 181

Maybe you're getting a second chance. Maybe you're getting another opportunity to clear the slate and begin again. Maybe the second part of your life begins after this crisis and maybe you're going to see the purpose in it all one day. Maybe once this is all over and you're back to breathing steadily, you will no longer take for granted any peaceful hour that comes into your being. Maybe there's something you're learning right now that can only be known in this way. Maybe there really is a purpose to what's happening, and maybe you'll see it all clearly soon.

DAY 182

Anything that goes unrequited is just unmatched energy. It's not about who is more worthwhile than who, what traits, baggage, or strengths tally up or take you down a few points, placing you in or out of the box of being loved or left. What it comes down to is that there is misaligned momentum, a way in which you are moving through the world that does not flow congruently to the way someone or something else is. This does not mean that either of your rivers are misdirected, but that sometimes, the idea of leaping onto another person's path can become an escape fantasy: an idea of how you might remove yourself from the inevitability of our own inner work. This is futile, of course, because often, the things we latch onto in an effort to avoid our own demons are the very ones that bring us right to them. Let go. You're attached to something that will never bring you fully to where you're meant to be.

DAY 183

Your love was not wasted on those who couldn't love you back. Rejection may be painful, but it's not indicative of your inability to connect. Your ability to love strengthens with practice, with time, with your clear willingness to offer love even to those least willing to receive it. Your journey, then, becomes one of discernment. It is not about how you love, but who.

20\\\120m

DAY 184

It is okay to unearth the seeds you have planted when you realize your garden is not harvesting what you need to grow. It is okay to begin again. It is okay to think differently, to want differently, to move differently through this world. Your journey is defined by how you tell the story, and by how willing you are to tell a new one when it's time.

DAY 185

If you are trapped in a pattern, if it feels like you are pushing against an ocean current that keeps carrying you back to shore no matter how hard you try to get to the other side—stand still. Look back at what you are running from and unpack it. Be in it, just for a moment. Evaluate, and question. It's probably not your strength that's lacking, but it may be your strategy. Sometimes, running into a wall does not mean you need to be strong enough to push through it, but wise enough to see that there is another way. Sometimes, you are being asked to find an easier way to be.

22 1 1 1 2033

D A Y   1 8 6

Your brain works against you in ways you don't realize. The compulsion to repeat makes familiar discomfort desirable. The negative is disproportionately focused on because it feels like a more clear potential threat. You are an evolving being trying to operate with pieces of a machine developed for the most blunt kind of survival. Your growth is the product of witnessing those impulses and choosing otherwise, again and again, until it is instinctive, until it is rewired. When you live from what's immediately comfortable, you miss out on what's infinitely beautiful: what exists beyond where the limits appear to be.

DAY 187

No two loves are repeatable because the chemical reaction between souls, the merging of little universes, makes a world all its own, a compound that cannot be recreated. The loss of that is unquestionably something to grieve, but sunsets never paint the sky in exactly the same shades again either. There are opportunities that will arrive at your door in the morning that won't come back in the afternoon. There are moments where you will gather just the right people, at just the right time in all of your lives, when there are enough common threads to bind you into a collective resonance that makes you feel safe and known. There are evenings where you will laugh your way through the moonrise, and you'll never be this young again. Yes, that love was incomparable, but there are other exquisite things, too. Find them. Let them engulf you.

DAY 188

Wisdom is the product of self-inquiry. Not time, as time is nothing but space that can remain empty and unused. Not experience, as life gone unevaluated has not been fully internalized, nor more deeply understood. Wisdom is the product of asking the hard questions as well as the simple ones. It is where our most gentle, child-like knowing meets the biggest parts of ourselves: the aspects of us that are willing to see the whole of our lives at once, and to remember what really matters, what is really worth investing our energy into.

25/11/2021

DAY 189

Your shimmering parts will feel the most vulnerable. The pieces of yourself that are so light and hopeful are the ones you will most want to clasp your hands around and protect. What you might not realize is that they are also the most impenetrable. What is unbendable can break with pressure, but what is effervescent within you—flowing, fluid, and flowering from the inside—never really leaves. It has the capacity to absorb shock and reground itself in its own knowing. It has no need to press back against criticism, but is instead nonreactive, knowing that there is no force outside of itself that can diminish it. There is nothing that can truly threaten it but your own unwillingness to let it simply be.

D A Y   1 9 0

You cannot force healing. You can only intend it, and then allow it. In the same way that every drop from a rainstorm must find its place upon the ground, every sensation in your body must be fully processed and released. This won't occur on your preferred timeline. It will come back in waves when you thought the waters were still. You aren't letting go of an experience, a person, or a place, but of all of the things you assumed you'd be, all of the things you made the loss mean about you, all the feelings that have to slowly unravel themselves so as not to overwhelm you. This takes time, so give that to yourself. What you gain from the process far exceeds whatever you think you lose in taking quiet refuge.

2.7·I·I·I·2O2J

DAY 191

Sometimes, the strongest thing in the world is to walk lightly when everyone is asking you to dig your heels into the ground and resist forward motion, to disregard the little things that light you up and make you feel something in favor of something more serious, more grave. Sometimes, the strongest thing in the world is to maintain your hope, your wild spirit, in a world that wants to extinguish it. Sometimes, your purpose in this world is not something you do, but someone you become. Someone you choose to be.

28/11/2021

DAY 192

Resistance feels like you're pushing away from something, but sometimes it's a sign you are being called to it more strongly than ever before. When something is a definitive *no*, you are clear and neutral and detached. When something is pulling at you at such a scale, you push back because you are afraid of losing control, of losing yourself within it. Sometimes, what you feel the most tension about is not what you are trying to push away, but what you are reaching to bring closer. What matters enough to scare you a little, is what you really, truly want.

25/11/2020

DAY 193

Allow the next era to begin. Give yourself a chance to try new things, to experiment, to wonder if maybe you were wrong. Let yourself contradict the older versions of yourself that you've outgrown. Do not apologize for changing your mind, do not let your ego shrink you backwards. Give yourself a chance to do the things you've always wanted, to become the type of person you've always admired. No, the journey is never seamless, but there is a specific kind of peace you find within when you are on your way to embodying a more aligned standard for yourself.

DAY 194

You are a field of contradictions, a constellation of experiences both painful and gorgeous, and all of the lingering hurts and shining possibilities that glisten in-between. You might want to define yourself by the most knowable parts, the cleanest and clearest self-concept imaginable, but the journey of true self-actualization is to embrace your juxtapositions. It is to hold them up to one another and understand that it is not always comfortable to consider the aspects of ourselves that complement and contradict each other, the pieces that don't fit, that don't make sense—but coming to grips with them is how you become the fullest version of yourself. It's how you set your entire life free.

01/12/2024

DAY 195

Passing judgment on others won't limit their potential, it will only set up a bar of expectation around your own. The thing about judgment is it appears to go outward, but it truly takes place inward. You create your own rules around what you deem acceptable or not, and then you must live by them. The more time you spend searching for reasons to invalidate another person's journey, the more you delay your own progress, your own growth. Healing is moving out from beneath the weight of your self-disapproval. It is unpacking the ways in which you've tied limiting beliefs around your concepts of the people around you, and recognizing how often your image of them was a projection of something you were unaware of within yourself. When you judge, you end up punishing yourself more than anyone, or anything, else.

D A Y   1 9 6

It takes a lot of heart to be who you are. It takes a lot of
courage to show your truest self to the world and be okay
with not being received by everyone, with not being seen.
It takes a lot of self-trust to stop adapting to tides that
come and go, but to stand firmly in who you know you are.
It takes a lot, and it matters a lot, because our self-concept
is the foundation of every single experience you have while
alive. It is the filter through which you come to know it all.
When you are firm within your truth, you may lose some
approval, but what will you gain? That is immeasurable.
Infinite. That is what it has always been about.

05/12/2021

DAY 197

Look yourself in the eye and tell yourself, *you're okay.* You're okay not because everything is perfect or went according to plan. You're okay not because every human being alive adores you, and you have never had an ounce of hurt in your heart. You're okay not because you know for sure what every hour of the future will hold. You're okay despite every reason you shouldn't be. You're still standing. You're still here, still soothing your inner storms, still searching for the answers, and still trying, even if your "try" only looks like being willing to make it through another night.

DAY 198

One day, you will see your own strength. You will begin to realize that the things that once pressed up against every nerve in your body are able to move through you with a little more ease. You will walk through the things you once most deeply feared, and you will walk out on the other side and be okay. You will realize that through what you face, you find your deepest courage—and you get to keep that with you for all the rest of your days.

DAY 199

Your energy will return; your love for life will once again pour out of you in all the smallest ways. You are not meant to be forever in an exhale, an expansion, a flow. There are some periods that are intended for taking it in, for contracting and clearing, for ebbing, and for learning something vital through those transits. When you begin to see yourself as an organic being you can give yourself more grace through your natural seasons. You are not meant to be flowering all of the time, and that is precisely what makes it so special, so sacred, when you do.

DAY 200

Do not allow your hope to be extinguished with time. No matter what this world might take from you, do not let it take your faith that another experience is possible, another chapter will begin one day, a new life can be formed from the ruins. If there is one thing that you must hold onto, it is only this—that change is not possible, it's inevitable. It can be different, and better, than it ever was before.

07/12/2021

DAY 201

You have so much more inside of you. I know that you feel depleted, and as though you are at the end of something. You are only at the end of the experience of being this one particular version of yourself. You have done all you could as the person you've been, and you're ready for the next phase of your evolution. You're ready to transform into a new person entirely, and you're going to discover pieces of yourself so deeply entangled in your being, ones you did not expect to live out. Give yourself space and time. New miracles are asking to emerge through the pain.

DAY 202

You might define yourself by your struggles, but others define you by your soul. You might not be able to see beyond your fears about yourself, but others see the beautiful things you bring into this world, the way you laugh and show up for the ones you love, and all of the lightness in who you are. Others see your gifts, your talents, and your kindness. Sometimes, you have to learn to see yourself with the grace of someone not so critically evaluating whether or not you deserve to be loved. You are love itself. Let it out, and let it be met, let it be taken, and let it be given back to you in even greater degrees.

DAY 203

After all the world has put you through, you are still here, holding your dreams up to the light. You are still here, asking for healing and change. You are still here, even if you have only an inch of hope left. You are still here because after everything the world has put you through, it has not extinguished what burns inside of you. It has not taken away your power to wonder if maybe another way is possible. And that? That will carry you all the way to the other side.

DAY 204

You will learn how to practice your own peace. You will learn what battles are worth fighting, and which aren't. You will learn how to hear your own intrusive thoughts and not believe them. You will learn how to confront a challenge and not assume your own failure, but instead try—actually try. You will learn that things do not improve surreptitiously, but as the result of practice. It doesn't get easier, but you become more resilient. You become more willing. You become better at bringing yourself back to your center and trying again.

11/12/2024

DAY 205

When you are in anger, say nothing. When you are in inspiration, run toward what's lighting you up inside. When you're in love, savor and share it, and make it known. You think that it's your thoughts and feelings alone that dictate and determine the climate of your soul, but it's really the actions those thoughts and feelings initiate that end up forming your reality. Learn to respond intelligently to what your emotions are asking, before they become erratic, loud, and seemingly out of control.

DAY 206

Learn to not over-complicate things. Allow things to be as they are, for people to be as they are. Sometimes, your desire to gaze beneath the experience isn't actually a mark of depth, but of skepticism, or a lack of faith. There are times in your life that are meant for introspection, and evaluation. There are times you are supposed to think critically about what it is you want to do and how you want to be. But there are also times to simply be in those experiences, to love and laugh and not worry about where it all will lead or what you're missing. Sometimes, true sophistication is the ability to just be present, and to let the rest just be.

DAY 207

The right ones lead you back to yourself. They remind you of all the pieces of yourself that went missing over the years. The right ones will make you more of the person you've always wanted to be: the person you've kept quietly inside you all along. The right ones will encourage you and inspire you, often without saying a word. The presence of their authentic selves awakens something that's so similar inside of you, you feel no choice but to rise up and allow it to blossom. The right ones teach you not through what they tell you, but simply by being who they are.

D A Y   2 0 8

You either see endings, or within them new beginnings. You either see that you're living the days your younger self once dreamt of or you're still waiting on something more. You either see a storm that disrupts your path, or one that corrects your course. You either see the hours as long and thankless, or life as brief and precious. You either see the mysterious unknown, or an endless realm of possibility. There is what you experience, and then there is the story you tell yourself about it. Over time, that story becomes the truth you carry, as the other details fade in the distance. Over time, how you write the narrative determines how you experience reality.

15|12|2021

DAY 209

It is a sacred thing to be sensitive, to feel deeply and let those emotions weld you into the wholest parts of who you are. To be willing to open up the deepest internal aspects of yourself, and to bring yourself to a new awareness each time. It is a sacred thing to embrace the parts of you that make you most human, that make you most honest and raw. It is a sacred thing to be able to feel a world many just move through. Don't ever let anyone take that away.

16112120<u>2</u>

DAY 210

Like most of us, what you are really working toward is
being able to have peace in the quietest, simplest moments
of the day. You can only get there by practicing again and
again, disengaging with the tempting thoughts that lead
you nowhere but self-destruction. You can only get there
by reacclimating to an entirely new way of walking through
your hours, becoming comfortable in the new life you've
carved out of the unknown. The ending is not a place you
arrive, it is a way you become.

17/12/200

DAY 211

There is an inevitability within certain things in your life—
certain things inside of you that will emerge no matter
where you are, who you're with, or what other paths you
come to choose for yourself. There are simply things that are
predestined, not because they're chosen for you, but because
they are alive within you asking to be born outward.

DAY 212

You came here to grow—not to acquire or accumulate, not to be perceived perfectly or attain every charm in the world. You came here to deepen, to let go. To tie loose ends, to give closure. To love; to love. Please remember this when it feels as though you want to grip tightly to the pieces of your life that fit seamlessly within the structure of success, of safety, of making it. You are a wild soul in a temporary form. You are here to explore and have a story all your own. Don't deny yourself that. Don't deny yourself adventure.

DAY 213

What if you learned to fall in love with the mysterious, the unknown, the unanswered? What if instead of being afraid of the answers you do not yet have, you adopt the perspective that you're waiting to discover something so profound, so gorgeous, so unknowable at this state? What if what you really want is to experience those answers in layers, one at a time? What if what you're really waiting for is for you to become the kind of person who can most deeply feel the things that are on the way, the kind of person who is truly ready?

DAY 214

You chase your happiness because you fear it is fleeting, but you grip onto your pain with the belief that it will somehow become an everlasting part of your life. The root of this is the idea that your stasis is discomfort, when it is actually your own inner peace that you always come home to, that you always return to, that always reemerges no matter how far you wander. The fears you wrap around your feeling states that lead you to resist them come from a fundamental misunderstanding of who and how you really are. Let it hurt and let it pass. Let it teach you something on the way out. And when you do wake up once again in peace, remember that storm clouds pass through an evergreen sky, even when the light is gone for a while. It always clears. It always comes back. You always return.

DAY 215

You think the journey is becoming enough for other people,
but it is actually learning to be enough for yourself. It is
learning what you need and what you don't, what fills you
and what doesn't, who clicks with you and whose energy
does not harmonize with your own. You are allowed to draw
lines, to decide and to determine what fits you. You do not
exist to adapt to other people's needs. You are a universe
all your own.

DAY 216

I hope you press up on the boundaries of what you thought was possible, and I hope you go beyond them. I hope you let fear lead you to the most treasured, sacred, important parts of your journey. I hope you connect, first and foremost to yourself. I hope you do not let this life pass you as a series of certainties, as a checklist you're simply working through. I hope you truly live. I hope you let the living surprise you. I hope you come out on the other end better than you ever thought you could be.

23/12/20

DAY 217

An honest heart is rare. A heart that is willing to be earnest, and sincere. A heart that is strong enough to keep loving, no matter how many times it has been bruised. Irony and cynicism are shields, a way to laugh off your life so that it cannot truly touch you. This slowly ices you out to your own experience until one day you wake up and realize you are surrounded but lonely, busy but disengaged. If you want a full life you have to be willing to open yourself to it. Let it all in and let it move you. Let it change you. Let it free you and let it make you feel again. Let what's heavy hurt and what's healing lighten, and let yourself move through it all without getting too attached. You're here for a reason, and an understanding of that reason can only be dissected through your experience.

24|12|20

DAY 218

There are elements of who you will be one day that will form as a result of your experiences right now. You get to decide which way they shape you, whether they make way for a deepening within you, or scars you around the edges leaving you barely able to reach beyond your own hiding space. You get to decide what you do with the hurt, what you do with the hope, what you do with everything that finds you and leaves. You get to decide who you're going to be.

25/12/12026

DAY 219

I hope you learn to see yourself with kinder eyes. I hope you learn that your days do not have to be filled with everything the world says they must be. I hope you find the beauty in letting yourself rest, in letting yourself be. I hope you will nurture yourself in the simplest ways, I hope you will give yourself the benefit of the doubt. I hope you will see your strengths a little more than your weaknesses. I hope you know that you are more than you let yourself believe.

DAY 220

Of all the vast improbabilities that had to align for you to be here in this exact form, at this exact moment, in this exact place, meeting and feeling something deeply with only few souls out of the billions you could have come across—well, I hope it makes you believe in something. Even if you can't name what that something is, I hope it makes you realize how rare and irreplicable this moment is. I hope it makes you trust that maybe there's more to the gravitational pull that keeps all the planets in orbit— maybe there's a pull within that brings you directly to where you are meant to be.

27|12|2001

DAY 221

You were never meant to control other people's emotional experiences and perceptions. You were meant to find integrity within yourself. To find your own peace. Do you aim to focus your attention on how your life affects others' without realizing that a heart at home within itself acts with love? It is your inner alignment that you must tend to first and foremost. Turning inward is not an act of selfishness, but the first act of true kindness. It is only when you realize that you must calm your own storms that you stop pushing rain upon other people in your life.

DAY 222

Traces of the future line the history of your life. You will come to see that the years will invariably lead to a zenith moment when all of the loose ends find one another in the most mysterious and serendipitous of ways. Trust that there is a calling upon your life, and no experience, no matter how painful or confusing, will be wasted in the end.

DAY 223

How do you know what to do next? You ask yourself, honestly, what your 90-year-old self would advise you to do. What they would have wished you had done. You ask yourself, honestly, what you've sensed from the beginning. What you have ignored, what you have quieted and distracted yourself from. You make two lists, the positives and the negatives, and you weigh them. And if there is one thing on the left that overpowers the dozen things on the right, then you trust that. You ask yourself what path will make you more of the person you are meant to be.

DAY 224

Some of the very best parts of your life begin to flow right after you give up. After you give up on trying to be someone you're not, in placing other people's opinions higher than your own. After you stop trying to live out the plan that you have outgrown, after you stop trying to make the wrong pieces fit. Sometimes, holding on isn't about muscling through, but knowing what you are meant to release along the way.

DAY 225

At the end of the day, we are all looking for a soft place to land, arms that want to hold us, and someone who is willing to listen. We all just want to be loved, we all just want to be known. Remember that when you are struggling to understand someone. Find compassion. We are not so different on the inside, although the surface may tell a different story.

DAY 226

With how much detail can you describe the antennae of a flower, or the sunset, or the best night of your life? With how much understanding can you explain the ways in which you overcame your greatest challenges? How deeply do you know yourself? Your life enriches as you expand your ability to describe and understand the processes and intricacies of what it is to be alive. Pay attention. There's more here than you realize.

01/01/2024

DAY 227

Heed the inner calls. The little nudges, the quiet voices that direct your vision toward the next place you're meant to be. These forms of guidance are not always so clear. They are subtle, because they are still seeds. They are still undirected, unactualized potential. Listen to them, and ask about them, and let them show you the way to the place on the planet where they may come to be.

DAY 228

How do you figure out what you really want? You imagine a life that would be too good to be true, and then you take note of the elements, the themes. Are you surrounded by others, are you quiet? Are you hopeful, or healing, or resting? Are you adventuring, are you in your wild? Are you creating, are you more unique? The picture does not have to come fully into fruition for you to understand that its pieces are directing you to the most honest aspects of yourself. Make a map of that life and live it now. Live it here.

04/01/2024

DAY 229

Just because it is not happening in
the timing you expected
does not mean it is not happening.

DAY 230

The parts of your journey where you felt like you were failing and falling behind, the moments when it seemed like nothing was working out the way it should, the times during which you were all but forced to prioritize rest, to begin a process of self-reflection, to have no choice but to change—these weren't your setbacks, they were your break-throughs in disguise. The universe is constantly asking if you are ready to stop engaging with your old habits and enter into a parallel life, one you begin to build in the gaps between what happens and how you respond. The next time you are faced with the exact same challenge, you are being called to ask: *how can I respond differently this time?*

06101 12024

DAY 231

Sometimes, your hardest pivots are rerouting you to your greatest destinies. Sometimes, you are growing through the most unlikely circumstances, the most confusing experiences. Sometimes, when it seems like you are falling behind with the outside world, you are actually coming into alignment with your internal one—finally listening to the deeper, inner wisdom that's telling you that you are meant to move beyond everything you've known into something bigger than you'd ever fully let yourself believe.

DAY 232

You are growing, even when it feels like you are doing nothing but being still. You are growing, even when it feels like you are doing the opposite of moving forward, when it feels like all you can think about is what you regret, what you wish you had done differently, the way you think it all should have unfolded. Within disappointment is great knowledge, if you have the courage to look at your life beyond the perspective of your ego, the part of you that is so intent on seeking evidence to affirm its perceived inadequacy.

081011202Y

DAY 233

One day, life will show you what was waiting on the other side of the storm. One day, life will show you that it had a plan for you all along, even amid your deepest doubt that anything beautiful could be born of the mess. One day, life will show you that your quietest hopes were the outline of your deepest destiny. One day, life will show you the purpose of the pieces that fell apart and what came together in their place. One day, life will show you that you can trust in the progression, the evolution. One day, life will show you that it was always on your side.

DAY 234

Maybe your constant wanting of more is not evidence that you are insatiable with your desire for the material aspects of this world, but because your true needs are not being met. Because there are ways in which your life is not functioning the way you want and need it to be, because there are ways in which you're missing connection. The fabric of your days is fraying and you do not know how to sew it back together. Maybe your constant wanting is actually a symptom of what's not yet been fully seen. The truth is that you can never have enough of what you do not actually need. You can never have enough of what does not fill the hole inside.

10101/2024

DAY 235

Your life begins the day you are willing to toss aside the ancient blueprint of what you thought would be and witness instead what is in front of you and use it. To hold it. To make the very most of it. Because your younger self, in all of your dreamy-eyed wonder and naivety, could not conceive of a life for an adult that you did not yet know how to have. No, you're not giving up, you're giving in. Into your flow, into your potential, into what's here, now.

DAY 236

Your existence only has to feel meaningful to you. It is beautiful in the smallest ways. Sometimes, the weight of your dissatisfaction comes from the crashing down of all the perspectives you've heard and held within, what you've tried to measure up to, as if one sunrise could compete with the next, one flower could blossom more perfectly than the next, one field of grass could flow with the wind in a more perfect pattern. If you can manage to make one perfect moment, one fleeting second, within this day—you have achieved more than you can imagine. You have awakened your soul.

210112024

DAY 237

Let the seams unravel and reform your entire life the way you really intend for it to be. When you are forced to let go, you are also asked to exhale. What does not hold is not meant to. If you are not certain, wait. Time reveals all truth, all knowing, all reality that will come to be. It will all become clear.

DAY 238

Your life is a collaboration with the gods, with the ions that made you, with the winding histories that led to this precise millisecond in time, and you think you're not here for a reason? The vast improbability that you could come to be in your precise form, with all of your interests and gifts intersecting over this singular space where you can nurture the garden of humanity's soul in some small way that's only yours, and you think you're not here for a reason? Go outside and gaze up at the galaxy around you. This is an irreplaceable moment in time.

DAY 239

You came here to know what could only be known in human form, what could only be touched by two hands, seen with two eyes, felt in one body. Your soul wants a body to do what only bodies can. To turn dreams into carbon and nitrogen and oxygen. To love in solely human ways. To play with matter as though it were malleable and unformed, waiting for you to sculpt it. To witness the coexisting creators and all they come to be. To discover, to learn—not only about you, but the tiny, golden thread that connects you to any and every other being and thing. There is a purpose in this imperfection. There is a reason why you're here.

D A Y   2 4 0

You have no idea how not alone you are. You have no idea how many other people walk through this world with similar thoughts, and fears. How many people have felt the sinking, crashing weight of heartbreak, the hope of the future, wondering if they did it all wrong. The optics can be deceiving. It is easy to feel alone. You are not alone. *You have no idea how not alone you are.*

18101120UL

DAY 241

A greater wisdom exists at the helm of your internal compass, always guiding you—sometimes gently, sometimes abruptly, and sometimes without you even realizing it at all. Could you imagine if you lived your life knowing that the voiceless, intuitive sense within you was guiding you to something within but beyond this life? To joys you don't yet know exist, to forms of happiness you wouldn't have been able to imagine? What if all the discomfort within you is simply trying to get you to move in another direction? What if the very things you want are hidden behind the very things you fear? What if there's a plan for you bigger than you can understand? Can you learn to trust yourself? Can you have faith in what your heart knows, but your eyes have not yet seen?

DAY 242

I hope you will begin to realize how powerful the mechanism of your mind is: how your stream of consciousness is offering you a glimpse into a realm of possibilities, and it is what you choose, and what you return to, and what you begin to believe in, that will transpire in the most surprising and beautiful ways. When thought meets intention, and intention meets feeling, and feeling meets choice, and choice meets action, and action meets consistency, and consistency meets time, you can build your way into an experience you previously didn't even know was possible.

18 01 2024

DAY 243

You really can change. You can change because you were designed for it. But you're never going to if you keep spending your time running into the same walls trying to overpower your resistance rather than asking it what vulnerable part of yourself it's trying to protect. When you don't listen to yourself you go to war with yourself, both by trying to force your way and by giving up, by assuming that your first approach is the only one available. Learn from your resistance and your pain. The lesson comes to us not from life, but through living.

DAY 244

You will be guided to exactly what you need, and not a moment before you need it; exactly who you're meant to love, and not a moment before you're meant to know them; exactly where you need to be, and not a moment before you need to be there. Trust your journey. It may seem as though it's operating on some kind of chaotic timing, but in truth, you become aware of potential experiences as you are ready to have them. Sometimes, it's not the world you are waiting on, but yourself.

20/01/2024

DAY 245

You have to decide what you're willing to miss out on. Will you be the artist missing nights of sleep, working after their day job? Will you miss being out with your friends, will you miss your potential, will you miss the world, will you miss the safe space you've called home? The truth is that every decision comes with a parallel sacrifice of some sort, something you won't know and can't know. As much as you have to decide what's worth trying for, you also have to decide what's worth letting go of.

21/01/2024

DAY 246

On the days when it feels like you will never get through this season, this period, this transition—please remember all of the mountains you have scaled before. Please remember all of the nights you spent convinced that you'd never move beyond where you were until finally something small brought you a little ease, and then a little more. You waited. You realized that everything was going to be okay, even if it doesn't always feel okay. You let the waves of all those big feelings crash over you, and then you let them recede. You found courage. You did things you once did not believe you could do, finding the will to wake up and face another day. You found softness. You found yourself. You found forms of love you never expected, and you began to appreciate what you couldn't see before. You began to feel like you were enough because you decided what would be enough for you. You developed resilience. You explored the perimeters of what your heart could hold, and how much it could process. You discovered that your strength is limitless, a truth you often don't know until you are tested, until you are asked to dig it out from beneath your doubts, fears, and false beliefs. Over time, what once seemed impossible became ordinary. The life you have today is a mere dream of the past. The things you do right now were once the things you prayed to have. Please, do not forget that when you most fear the future. Each time you have stepped forward, the road rose to meet you—and it will again.

DAY 247

Everything changes when you shift from attempting to force outcomes to attracting the very particular things that are meant for you. It's a surrender, allowing a butterfly to sit gently on your shoulder, to bond with you, to become yours not because you need them to be, but because some force just beyond you has bound you in a way you cannot logically explain or describe. That's the magic you're looking for. Your focus moves magnetism into your top priority, to become the strongest, clearest, kindest possible version of yourself, honing the skills that are uniquely yours. Your priority becomes deeply caring for yourself in the most sincere ways. What you don't realize is that when you are nurtured, it changes the way you interact with the world around you. It changes what's attracted to you. The things that are meant for you are drawn to you when your light is on, so focus on turning it on. When you live like this, you find what you're looking for in ways you didn't even know you were looking for it to show up.

DAY 248

It is time to take your life back. The life you lost to fear, the life you lost to the opinions you valued over your own happiness. The life you lost because it couldn't fit within the image that the world has made you think is ideal. The life you lost because you came to believe you were not worthy of your own joy, your own path, your own truth. The life you lost because you put it on hold, hid it behind a *someday*, a *maybe*, a *should be*, a *would be* if only you found the courage to take even the smallest step toward the path you know is yours.

24|01|2024

DAY 249

The resistance within is brilliant. It knows every terrify-ing thought you have ever had and every fear to play on. It knows what you will respond to, what will seduce you, what will scare you into staying frozen. You must learn not to allow fear to rob you of your life. You must learn not to project your perception of limitation onto a limitless world. You must learn that you exist far and beyond the opinion you have of ourselves, and maybe, just maybe, if you stopped to look around, you'd realize that you are far more brave, far more powerful, far more beautiful, and far more loved than your smallest self would let you believe.

DAY 250

How do you heal when it won't stop hurting? You let yourself rest. You let yourself rest for longer than you think is reasonable, and you do not let yourself feel one second of guilt for that. You go as easy on yourself as you possibly can. You nurture yourself in the simplest, most honest ways. You do the bare minimum and accept that on days like these, that is more than enough. You stop imposing a timeline. You stop extrapolating this one moment and allowing it to overtake your entire self-concept. You have smiled, and you will again. It has been good, and it will be again. You may forget this in your lowest moments, but what really matters is that you validate where you are at; what matters is that you make sure it's not only the acceptable parts of you that get seen.

DAY 251

Some feelings ask you to overcome your most basic instincts in favor of a higher road. Some feelings ask you to see within others what you are quietly suppressing within. Some feelings ask you to just be with them. Some feelings ask you to move, to change, to become. Some feelings ask you to remember how easy it is to suffer, and others remind you that peace is always a possibility if you can train your mind to quiet itself enough to perceive it. What makes you human is your ability to decide. When you respond to every emotion without reflecting on whether it's coming from fear or truth, you are controlled by an outside world you misperceive as an internal one. When you utilize intellect and your ability to discern, you evolve to see them both as one.

DAY 252

Now, now, now. It's all happening now. Everything. All of it. Every joy, every sorrow. The planting of every seed and the blooming of every flower. The sunrise on one side of the world and the sunset on the other. Every memory, every projection, every hope, every fear—all stemming from the forever now. What if it is not that you cannot understand your past or imagine your future, but that you have not yet learned how to be here, now, now, now: the single stage where all of time unfolds? What if the journey was really always about learning how to be in it, be with it, here, now? It's now, now, now. Now or never, now or no time at all. It's only ever now. What will you do with your now?

28101120<u>24</u>

DAY 253

You have no idea how many versions of yourself you've already shed. How many beliefs, once so tightly held, were unwound with new evidence, with time, with heart-opening, mind-altering willingness to be a little more human than you were before. You'll release this version of you, too, but there will be common threads you will carry with you throughout them all—look for those. Look for what remains true. That is who you really are.

DAY 254

You don't have to figure your entire life out today.
Show up a little more as the person you want to be.
Tomorrow, do it again.

01/01/2024

DAY 255

Do not retire your daydreams. Everything that exists originated within someone's mind, a mind that first had to believe in its own idea enough to make it real. You might not see it in front of you yet, but if you feel it within, you have the capacity to bring it to life. Bridging the space between what you envision and what you actually experience is the journey of your life.

DAY 256

If it is truly meant for you, it will come back to you. If it is truly meant for you, it will leave only for the sake of teaching you the lessons you could only learn on your own. If it is truly meant for you, it will return even if you've pushed it away, even if you're in denial, even if you assume something so beautiful could never be truly yours—because if it is truly meant for you, it is never not a piece of you. It is never not intricately tied into the depths of your soul. If it is truly meant for you, the path you take when you turn away from it will be the road that leads you to it. If it is truly meant for you, it is already waiting for you to arrive.

01102122024

DAY 257

How do you believe in your potential when your reality tells a different story? You begin to understand that belief is not found; it is built. It is built from desire, from hope, from passion morphed into some tangible reality. You begin to understand that the nature of your conviction is not some transient emotion that holds no weight nor meaning but rather a directional impulse that keeps pointing in the exact same direction. You begin to understand that the very nature of potential is that it is greatness not yet expressed. You become less interested in why it is not mysteriously manifesting itself and more curious as to what steps you could take to reimagine yourself in the light of what you really know you are..

02|02|2024

DAY 258

The leap of faith is when you step away from what's
good in pursuit of what could be extraordinary.

DAY 259

When you observe something for too long, you inevitably discover every microscopic fault line within it, and when you focus for too long on those minor imperfections, you begin to piece together an image of that thing as being fundamentally flawed. Introspection can function similarly. It is good to go inward, but only if you also spend enough time moving outward—seeing, feeling, experiencing new things. If you spend your life picking yourself apart, you will find more than enough to be dissatisfied with. Rest your eyes and your mind, and let your heart settle. When you think of yourself again, you will do so with more kindness, more grace. You will realize that nit-picking your soul is not growth; it is resistance. It is a denial of the beautiful truth of all that you have come to be.

DAY 260

I hope you will take nothing for granted—no lesson, no person, no place. I hope you will see that everything was a teacher, even the most unlikely of experiences was in some way there to guide your path. I hope you will have faith in the fact that everything that's meant for you will find you, remain with you, or return to you. It is only a matter of when. I hope you will realize that when you ask for a bigger experience, you'll first be handed the lessons that will grow you into the type of person who can have that life you envision. I hope you'll begin to see the purpose in what's seemed meaningless. I hope you'll never lose faith that your happy ending is still there, still waiting.

DAY 261

You hold yourself back when you are too hard on yourself. In the space of self-punishment, you leave no room for learning. You hold yourself back when you believe you are alone. You are not so different deep inside, though the functioning of the current world requires you to believe that you are. You hold yourself back when you don't trust yourself, when you give up after the first few tries, when you stop thinking in terms of possibility. You hold yourself back when you do not give yourself the grace to grow.

DAY 262

Go, because it does not serve you to live beneath the weight of all the lives you could have lived. Go, because if a dream still lingers within you year after year, it is not an escape, it is a calling. Go, because if you get to the end only to discover you preferred where you were at the beginning, the doors never close on the places destined for us. If it's truly for you, it will always be waiting. It will be a homecoming, one way or another. Go, because one day you won't have the time left. Go, because there will always be another reason not to. Go, because while you can measure everything you might lose, you cannot yet see all you may gain. Go, because everything beautiful and secure that exists around you right now is simply proof of what you're capable of creating, not a singular moment of goodness that will never exist again. Go, because anything that pulls you is worth pursuing. Go, because there is nothing more risky than ending this story with a heart full of regrets.

07|02|2024

DAY 263

When it's right, it will give you as much energy as it takes. It will inspire you and motivate you and encourage you as often as it challenges you and pushes you and scares you. When it's right, what you reach for will reach back toward you. When it's right, it will blossom without you having to force it. When it's right, it will help you become more of the person you're meant to be, not distract you from your own growth. When it's right, it will flow spontaneously and serendipitously, and it will guide you through a series of coincidences too meaningful to truly be coincidental. When it's right, you'll look back and realize that all the steps you took were leading you right to this one, that the signs were really there all along.

DAY 264

You will resist your own growth. You will resist your own growth because you were taught that what's most familiar is most worthwhile. You will resist your own growth because you came to believe letting go is a loss when it is in fact a beginning. You will resist your own growth because you do not yet know that nothing presses us to release it unless something else is imminently waiting to arrive. You will resist your own growth in the same way a seed must break through its own shell before it can take root, in the same way the darkest hour of the night is the one before the first light of dawn meets the horizon. You will resist your own growth until you learn that growth is all there is, and when you try to stop your own evolution, you stand in the way of every beautiful thing you intend to experience. You will resist your own growth because it is scary to grow, but slowly you will realize, it is far scarier not to.

09102/2024

DAY 265

What if the real growth, the real journey, the real glow up, was when you stopped waiting until you transformed into the most flawless version of yourself, and instead began to care for the person you are right now? What if it was never about whether or not you could push away all of the parts of yourself you don't feel are enough, but instead to be able to hold them all, to allow them to coexist? Can you imagine the doors that would unlock for you if you stopped fighting battles you cannot win, if you stopped viewing every aspect of yourself as amendable, shiftable, movable? What if part of your destiny is also discernment, the ability to see the difference between the parts of yourself that need to be worked on, and the parts of yourself that need to be seen, embraced, and known?

DAY 266

Sometimes, your simplest visions are your most honest ones, your most sincere truths. Not the most impressive story, not a world-defying feat of humankind, not a dream so extreme and singular that it would take a lifetime of devotion to achieve. Rather, the dreams that make you feel it's safe to exhale. The dreams that signify a life kindly lived. The dreams that make you feel as though you're finally going home. Those ones? Find them, and run to them—they are your truths most deeply held.

1102(2024

DAY 267

Maybe healing isn't so much about changing, but remembering. Remembering who you are, how you really want to be. Learning to use what you have, to care for your life in the most human ways. Maybe it is about learning to come home to yourself, to create warmth within your own chest, to let your love pour out of you and touch everything around you. Maybe it was never about waiting for someone else to show up and make it all okay, but realizing that you've had that power inside you all along.

DAY 268

Every step in the right direction is itself a victory.

Every step in the right direction
makes you a little more free.

1/10/2/2024

DAY 269

If it does not lead to more peace in your life, it is not in alignment. If it does not lead to a deeper place within yourself, it is not in alignment. If it requires you to sacrifice your values and gives you an unsettled feeling in your stomach, it is not in alignment. If it requires you to be dishonest with anyone, even yourself, for a prolonged and complex period of time, it is not in alignment. If it does not give you space to grow and change, it is not in alignment. If it does not make you a better human being, it is not in alignment.

DAY 270

If you're going to judge yourself by anything, do it by how bravely you weathered emotional storms. Do it by how many imperfect hearts you've loved, you've seen nothing but goodness within. Do it by how many times you've laughed until you've cried, how many times you've been the best kind of friend. Do it by how many times you've faced your fears and got up again despite it all. If you're going to judge yourself, don't do it by what you had to do in order to get by, don't sum yourself up by what you did to heal. You are so much more than what you've survived.

DAY 271

How do you stop worrying? You realize that the power you need to get through absolutely anything is dormant inside of you and will not be activated until the moment you need it; the version of you that will walk you forward will be born in the doorway of the moment you need them. You are not meant to contain within yourself every possible version, every iteration, of who you might one day be. You do not have to embody the fighter and the lover and the healer and the maker all at once. There is a time for everything, a season for each. The human spirit is the fiercest weapon on the planet and the force of all of nature is inside of you. It will be awakened when you call upon it, and not a second prior.

DAY 272

Nobody, not even the most seamlessly put together, ambitious, strong, popular, and healthy ones among us know exactly what they are doing. We are all wandering through this dreamscape, trying to find our purpose, trying to make our way. If you could come to see the things that pain you as not unique to your own faults and rather a simple element of the human condition, you could show yourself so much more kindness, so much more grace. It would be so much easier to move through life knowing you are not meant to be anywhere more than where you are right now, and the next place you arrive to will be just in time, too.

17|02|2024

DAY 273

Right now, you are learning how to live. You are learning what feels right and what doesn't, what you like and don't, who you want to be. You are learning how to become yourself, how to make it through your days without letting your spirit wear down. Right now, you are learning how to be. How to exist in the quiet, in the questions, in the faith of everything that has not yet come, but surely one day will arrive. Right now, you are learning how to love. Yourself today, your past self and the person you'll one day be.

DAY 274

Walk as though your destiny could arrive at the door to meet you at any given moment—because it can, because it will. Because none of us can perfectly predict the timing of how anything will unfold, but when you live with the expectation that good things are coming, they tend to arrive one way or another. They tend to find you no matter where you might be.

19|02|2024

DAY 275

If you are allowing your life to be controlled by your fear of other people's perceptions of you, it would serve you to ask yourself who those people are, to put faces to their names, and to discover that your abstract fear is a blanket for specific rejections: ghosts that are still holding something over you. The love of those who do not fully approve of us seems most appealing when our own self-concept is laced with self-rejection. It feels familiar, it seems to align. You must learn to practice self-approval, to give yourself the benefit of the doubt, to show up with the humble knowing that you might be imperfect, but you are trying. You are doing the best you can. You must begin to see yourself through the eyes of someone who loves you. That is the first step of healing. Then you must learn to stop projecting altogether, and regain your own perspective—not to believe you are as you imagine you're seen, but to simply witness what's in front of you, allowing the rest to fade away.

DAY 276

Let yourself be changed by the love in your life. By the beautiful mornings, by the souls who want to meet you where you are. By all the opportunities that emerged out of impossibilities, for every way in which the path unfolded even when you most feared it wouldn't. By how tremendously you have grown, and healed, and come so far. Let yourself be moved by all the goodness that surrounds you. You have so much more than you can currently see.

21 02 2024

DAY 277

You aren't going to be able to think your way out of fear, because fear is an irrational force. You will have to leap with your heart racing, again and again, until you have carved out a new comfort zone in the arena of your deepest desires. You will have to learn to live with it, the invisible thing within you that wants to shield you from anything unknown. You will have to learn to speak to it, to comfort it, but above all, to defy it. Again and again, until you have built within you a new home.

DAY 278

The moments when you want to turn away from yourself, to distract and numb it all out—those are the very ones where you most need to go inward. The ones where you most need to nurture yourself, to hear yourself out. When you're processing pain, one of the most healing things you can experience is the presence of someone to witness you, and to validate you—and there is nobody who can do that more powerfully than you. To believe in your story, to honor where you are on the journey—it is priceless, it is life-changing. You stop seeking external forces to tell you what you already know, and you begin to build an internal rapport. You begin to re-parent the part of yourself that wants to be heard and seen and felt. You begin to understand what you really need because for the first time someone is actually listening. You're actually hearing what your internal self is telling you it wants to be.

2)|02|2024

DAY 279

Life contains within it an invisible fullness, a way of being that puts you in the arena, no longer an idle witness to the happenings around you. This fullness, it's not something you can reach toward, it's something you have to open up inside of you, something that awakens in you after you've been gutted down to your core. You think that any way in which life has broken your heart has diminished your capacity, when in fact it often heightens it. It is the heart that has lost that knows love. That is the terrible, gorgeous truth of being human—you are grown into more completeness for the ways in which you have been challenged, and the ways in which you have been changed. Life enriches itself as it reveals to you its contrast. You do not truly appreciate what you have never had to live without, what you have never had to try for. You will never receive answers to the questions you never asked.

DAY 280

The most magnetic force you will ever possess is the power to be your true self. Things align, and click, and work a little more effortlessly than they did before. You progress by leaps and bounds because you are no longer being held back by the little voice in the back of your head telling you that *this isn't it*. You unleash the full capacity within you because something deep inside knows this is what your energy is meant to be spent on. This is what you're meant to be doing with your life. These revelations do not always occur instantly or easily, but they are always foreshadowed: hinted upon over the years. You can always trace the pieces back to their origin points, the genesis moments when you uncovered the littlest pieces of what the future would be. Open your heart to what flows when you touch it. It will revolutionize your entire world.

DAY 281

The beginning of all things is an idea, held and revisited, again and again, until the details come into form. Nothing is possible at the onset—it's all speculative, it's all a vast day-dream. Then, once the vision is considered for long enough, the ideation begins to feel like a memory not yet passed—a sister life, a congruent reality not yet known. Your work is not to allow the brain to skim over the impossible, but to access it by placing your hands down into the day and pulling out of it that very vision. You make real what you meditate on long enough to bring to life.

26|02|2024

DAY 282

When you are a child, your bones ache while they stretch and you come into the full form of who you are going to be. But they do not grow forever. It isn't always that hard. Your soul development is similar. Eventually you settle into who you're going to be and then your job is to be them as well as you can. Eventually you find yourself. Eventually you decide. You were not built to sustain a constant trial and error, a constant search for truth. You don't always grow from the constant influx of new information and input and experience, but by focusing on the simplicity of the moment in front of you, the study of the person you currently are and not just the one you may one day be.

DAY 283

Can you imagine if you truly spent the rest of your years just trying to compensate for the things you were never supposed to be good at, cultivating and maturing your weaknesses? *Mature your strengths.* Find what you are good at and get better, not because you are racing toward some imaginary finish line but because fate is a practice, a commitment to take the raw potentiality alive within us and to fall in love with it, to make something of it, and to offer it. Offer it far and wide and to anyone who wants to receive it. The gift is not what we're given, but what we're meant to give away.

DAY 284

Eventually, there will be a dream planted in your heart that seems beyond your capacity to hold, beyond your ability to manifest. That is when the journey of your life will begin. The journey into trust, into surrender, into stepping into the person that you need to be. You will realize, at the end, that the point wasn't really whether or not you ever arrived but who you became in the process. Because that person? They're here for more than just that one, singular vision that lit you up and fueled you all the way to where you'll one day stand. That person is your true self, finally revealed. The dream is the one piece of them that you can currently see.

29\02\2024

DAY 285

In the end, we are all just seeking the courage to love what we really love. To choose what makes us truly happy. Not what is enough, not what we only need to survive, not what other people would say is the ideal. In the end, we are all just seeking the heart to decide our own lives, on our own terms.

DAY 286

Each artist begins with a blank canvas, each musician the same octaves of notes, each writer the same dictionary of words. Mastery is not about the material, but what you do with it. What you create upon it. How you piece and stitch and weave it together and create something that is at once completely new to your human self and the embodiment of home to your soul. That is what you are longing for, after all. The things that make you remember who you really are.

DAY 287

What is written in the stars is seeded in your heart—but it is what you nourish with the light of your awareness that you will bring forth into reality. No matter how deep your potential, in the end, you become what you give the most attention to.

DAY 288

Piece by piece, you are going to make a life for yourself. Not because you have finally arrived at a place where everything is perfect, but because you have allowed your flowers to grow in between the concrete of your grief. Because you have chosen to believe in hope for just one more second than you have indulged your fear. Because you learned to stop holding yourself to your own impossible standards and began to practice following your heart through each hour of each day, letting it lead you to the greatest revelations, smallest pleasures, and the quiet salve of healing hours. You are going to make a life for yourself, even if you fear you're not. You've been doing it all along.

04/03/2024

DAY 289

Do not underestimate the power of making time for grounding yourself, for preserving your sanctity of mind in the most unassuming ways. Sometimes, starting the day with a moment of quiet rather than immediately reaching for your phone can be enough to reinforce how important it is to delineate your attention more carefully. Sometimes, changing what you see, smell, or hear can awaken parts of you that have been dormant for so long, you have forgotten they existed at all. Begin here, with the things that seem impossibly obvious. Let them lead you into the revelations that become revolutions.

05/03/2023

DAY 290

Listen to the part of you that's quietly reaching for
something just out of your line of sight. Follow it into the
unknown and trust your most powerful inner guidance
system wouldn't keep asking you to leap if there weren't
solid ground waiting to catch you, if there weren't greater
loves waiting to meet you, if there weren't bolder experiences
waiting to find you. The desire to leap is the promise that
there's something on the other side.

08|00|2024

DAY 291

What inspired you in your heaviest chapter? What made you once again believe in love? What soothed you when your heart had sown itself into the recesses of your body, and what helped it heal? What made you come to know yourself better, what questions yielded the most striking response? What did you once not know to think of that is now a regular part of your mentality? What made you feel most clearly alive? What nearly killed you? What made you believe again, what helped you cry when the tears were so bound into your throat you feared you'd never be able to let go? What do you not yet know? What do you know for sure? What's making you into the person you're going to be?

DAY 292

There's no expiration date on your destiny. You might fall madly in love in the second half of your life. The past five years may have been unconsciously preparing you to create your greatest work of art. Every failure may have been a lesson that turned into a skill that will be needed to build the life of your dreams. There is no expiration date on what you're meant to do.

DAY 293

Choosing peace isn't always so gentle at the beginning. Sometimes, it's screaming out all of the pain that you've tucked so deep within yourself, as though you could hide it out of existence. Sometimes, it is finally setting a boundary. Sometimes, it is saying no. Sometimes, it is uprooting from everything you've ever known and beginning again where your soul finally feels free. No, choosing peace isn't always so kind at the onset. Sometimes, it's a hurricane that finally waters the deepest gardens of your soul.

DAY 294

The difference between the ones who are defeated by their challenges and the ones who are transformed by them is often whether the person moves toward their discomfort, or runs away from it—as it is the ones with the courage to go inward are often rewarded far beyond their wildest dreams.

DAY 295

You have been willing to see so much divinity in beings who have not shown you grace or goodness, and yet you have not given yourself the chance to fall in love with yourself. You have not opened up to the possibility that all that godliness you could perceive within another mortal being was perhaps a reflection of who you are, and not them. You have not really sat with that idea—that your love could make someone seem so much more vivid, so much more possible than they are. You have not really considered what it might do to your life if you became the object of your own affection, if you offered yourself your own love.

11/03/2024

DAY 296

In the end, we'd all tell our younger selves similar things. To enjoy it while it lasts, because it won't last forever. To not worry so much about what is outside of your control and devote yourself more deeply to what is. To take that risk you've always dreamt about, and to do it sooner than you think you're ready. That there is no such thing as being ready, there is only doing, and then the readiness emerges in the process. To love even if it confirms all your worst suspicions about the brutality of a human heart. To not sabotage the good things when they arrive. To love the ones you have while you have them. To be young, to just be.

12/01/2024

DAY 297

One day, you are going to look back on this time and understand the purpose in the timing, in the delays, in the choices you have to make. One day, you are going to look back on this time and realize that you were far closer to the breakthrough than you knew. One day, you are going to look back on this time and realize that the road did rise to meet you, as it always did before, and as it always will. One day, you are going to look back on this time and realize you were always right where you were meant to be.

12/03/2024

DAY 298

In the end, your life is not going to be summed up by how tepidly you grazed the surface, how little you tried, how ironic you were, how infrequently you opened up your heart. It is not going to be summed up by how many times you failed, but the one victory it was all building up toward. I know it is hard to imagine yourself out of succession with all the younger parts of you that do not align with the person you are becoming, but at the end of the day, those people will not be remembered. They will not be your final form, rather, stepping stones on the way to your becoming. Focus on that—the legacy you'll leave. Not how well you avoided the deep heart of life, but how bravely you dove into it, again and again, until you finally reached the other side.

14|10|2024

DAY 299

It might seem like you've been healing forever, but the truth is that the more you are able to simply sit, witness, and allow your feelings without trying to change them, the more you'll be able to process in real-time. You'll be able to go through your day aware of subtle bodily sensations and rather than getting totally sidelined by any given setback or disappointment, you'll experience the world differently— with more sharpness, more vividness, more expansiveness.

15100|2024

DAY 300

Steady your vision.
Where you repeatedly step becomes
where you ultimately land.

DAY 301

What if there were only sixty more holidays left in your life, or fifty more summers, or ten more times you'll wake up early enough to watch the sunrise? What if there were only fifteen more times you'll fall asleep listening to the ocean beat against the shore? What if you've already read your favorite book? What if you only have three more times to see someone you love? What if you only have one? How fast does that change things—to think that maybe you do not have forever, though it feels like you have so much longer to survive? How differently will your eyes set their gaze the next time you arrive at one of those sacred moments, those irreplaceable days? How much more will you pay attention? How much more will you see?

17|00|2024

DAY 302

You cannot force what is not working. You will not bloom where you cannot deepen your roots, where you feel unsettled within yourself, within the life you are trying to build. You cannot force anything to be right, you have to listen. Listen to how you're responded to, to how you fit. Your environment will be one of the single most important elements of your life's journey, and it's your job to plant yourself somewhere you can actually expand, you can actually connect, you can most easily step into the person you really want to be.

18/10/2024

DAY 303

Maybe your anger is not a result of some misfiring within your soul, but a place within you that desires a boundary to be set, a new baseline of thinking to be adopted and embedded and used. Maybe your anger is not an overreaction, but an equal one, a reasonable response to an unquestionable unfairness. Maybe your anger is not trying to burn through your life, but through you—to make you stronger where you were once too allowing, too accepting, too unwilling to stand up for what you know is right. Maybe your anger is not the lack of your spirit, but finally, at last, its presence arising, and asking to be seen.

DAY 304

You can be as prepared as possible and still be surprised by challenges you never could have seen coming. You can have not one plan in place and discover that what you find out along the way exceeds your wildest expectations. There's so much gained in the process. It's on the field of life that you learn how to play the game, not by waiting on the sidelines.

DAY 305

There will come a day when the ease is a little greater than the heaviness, when it feels just undesirable enough not to look backwards, not to unpack the details one more time. That compulsion to keep yourself pinned to the past will lighten, and you'll begin to walk forward with more ease. You will slowly begin to forget all those harrowing details that kept you up at night. You will lose touch with the people that are meant to drift away, and one day, you will think of them for the very last time—though you will not know it is the last. Your mind will fill with new ideas, new distractions, new plans. You will move on. You really will.

21/05/2024

DAY 306

Piece your life together with the things that inspire you—no matter how incongruently one appears to flow to the last. That is how you craft a masterpiece, an experience entirely your own. You do not model the framework of your life by the unique way someone else has carved a home out of this existence. You make it your own, bit by bit.

12|03|2024

DAY 307

You know how you're going to get everything you ever wanted? By being kind. To yourself, to everyone you come across. Even when you think they don't deserve it, even when you think you don't deserve it—because you will eventually realize that it's not your job to decide who is worthy of love. Become as kind as you can muster, as kind as you can imagine, as kind as you have the courage to be. It is the key that will unlock it all.

DAY 308

Do not remain loyal to your negativity as though befriending it might protect you from it. To desensitize yourself in this way is not a form of strengthening yourself—quite the opposite. You must cement your belief in yourself in a loving way, you must be able to hold the contrast within you up like two scales, and balance them. You must be able to see yourself honestly and focusing only on the bad? That's not honest. That's not whole. That's not who you are. Receiving disapproval from the outside only shakes us if there's something inside of us that is beginning to believe the same thing.

DAY 309

How do you know what you really want? You get still, you get quiet. You go for long walks and you spend nights by yourself and you turn off your phone and you listen. You move past that wall of fear that makes you want to cling to the noise of the world—which ensures you'll never really hear yourself. You do this often enough and the answers will emerge without you trying to yoke them out of your subconscious mind. In solitude, you see who you truly are, and then when you bring that self back to the world, you're distinctly different and unprecedentedly powerful. You have something that many others won't dare to reach into themselves to find. You figure out who you are first, and then what you want will become obvious in time.

25/00/2024

DAY 310

You are worthy of love because you are willing to love. That's all it takes. We often think love requires us to tally up all of our flaws and all of our strengths to see who matches up with who. We often think that if love does not transpire into something long-lasting, it's because we are in some way lacking something that would make us a more clear and obvious choice. Love almost never works like that. We connect with who we connect with. It's mysterious; it's a force from within us and beyond us and it rarely ever makes sense until we're reviewing it all in retrospect. Sometimes, our hearts and bodies know things before our brains can rationalize them, and one of the hardest things is to see if we will trust that, if we'll believe in that, if we'll pursue that. Sometimes, doors close even when we beg them to stay open because we are being protected from what we cannot yet see. We meet people, it's electric, and we can't understand why. Sometimes we are just not ready for that and that's okay, too. Sometimes, there's someone or something else waiting on the other side. Sometimes, we're not quite the people we need to be to sustain that level of connection. Love is not always linear.

DAY 311

All change comes slowly at first—so slowly, in fact, it can begin to seem as though it isn't happening at all. This is the way of it, though. This is the way new realities move through the density of all the dimensions that separate you from it. On their way over, they tend to test your conviction, they ask you to prove that you really want it, to show up for it, to begin even when you are not certain the end of the road will meet you. The minute you take the first step on the path you have imagined is the moment the path appears in totality. That is how it goes. Everything else is preparation for that first leap.

27/03/2024

DAY 312

The people who have not yet come to see their own envy as a signal to the spaces in which they are destined to excel will see your growth as a threat. Grow anyway. The people who have not yet reconciled their desire for deep change in life will see your changes through only the lens of fear. Change anyway. The people who have not yet found their voices will think yours is too loud. Speak anyway. The people who have not yet healed their wounds will find your wholeness naive. Rejoice anyway.

DAY 313

Whatever you do, don't be like them—the ones that have hurt you. Being like them does not make you safer, cooler, or more free. It does not make you more accepted. It does not make you better than before. It does not make you wiser, it does not move you forward in life. It soothes the wound that cannot rationalize how so much unkindness can exist in a heart. So, it becomes in part to understand it, and in part to defend itself against it. Don't be like them, whatever you do. It will bring you no closer to healing.

29|03|2024

DAY 314

You are often most afraid of what you are meant for—it is one of those funny little things about being alive. You are afraid of the unknown but life is almost nothing but a series of unknowns. You are afraid of change, and growth, when you are designed for nothing but. You are most afraid of love when you want it more badly than anything, most afraid of your own greatness when it's practically pressing out of our skin begging to be released. That is why facing your worst fears often leads you to your greatest growth. It's often behind that wall that you find what you had been searching for all along.

30/03/2024

DAY 315

A soul does not truly get lost—it is a mind, untrained and untamed, that gets tangled in its own thoughts. Your mind gets away from you, wrapped up in all the superimpositions of how the world would implore you to think, to see, to keep yourself as minor characters in your own story. A soul does not truly get lost—it is always right there, waiting for the mind to open once again and see it clearly, feel it wholly, be in it without repeating the same old story yet again.

01/03/2024

DAY 316

An under-stimulated mind is one of the most quietly dangerous human conditions. You exist with the fear of how you might be incapable of achieving what you desire, when the true barrier is figuring out what you want to work toward, what you want to fight for, what you want to use all of that untouched energy inside for. When that momentum has nowhere else to go, it has a tendency to turn inward on you, to make you question and doubt and feel as though something is fundamentally and irreparably wrong with you. The human mind needs to be challenged: it needs to be given questions to answer, solutions to find, and consistencies to familiarize itself with. Your journey is not what life is easiest or most direct, but what engages you at the fullest level. What makes you most actively, potently alive?

01/04/2024

DAY 317

In case you haven't considered it before, it is entirely possible to carry your teenage complexes into your adult life. It is entirely possible to reach thirty, or sixty, and still struggle with outdated insecurities and fears and thinking. We assume that time will make healing an inevitability, as though it will all be wiped away as our memories fade. That isn't always true. Sometimes, you have to go inside and fix it yourself. Sometimes, you have to actively and consciously choose to believe what your most mature self would—if for no other reason other than that there is nothing that would disappoint your inner child more than to learn they'd made it through all those decades and still the little voice inside of them was not yet their friend.

DAY 318

If you do not yet know what choice to make, then it is probably not time to make it. There is probably another area of your life that is asking to be nurtured, developed, and strengthened instead. New factors to your decision-making have not been introduced yet—you don't know what you don't know. There is a strong possibility that you are premeditating a future decision that will need to be made eventually, but not today. When that day does arrive, you will know what to do. You will know what to do because you spent this preparation period strengthening your sense of self, clarifying what it is you really want and what it is you really value in life. If you do not yet know what choice to make, then it is probably not time to make it. Give yourself space.

09/04/2024

DAY 319

To be truly alive is, in many ways, to embody a slowness of living. It is to stretch and savor the precious, little things. It is to create pockets of calm out of ordinary hours, and it is to be in them, completely. It is the ability to focus more intently on what's in front of you without your mind wandering to what isn't. It's the capacity to lean into the experiences you're given, realizing at last that they're not all good nor bad, but a warped mindset can make it seem so. You change as you shift your attention, as you redirect your focus toward the parallel realities you are one thought away from living.

DAY 320

Sometimes, you sabotage everything around you because you don't know how to ask to leave; you don't know how to say you're ready to go. You sabotage relationships because you think you aren't ready for them, even if you want to be. You sabotage opportunities because you don't really want them, even if you think you should. Sometimes, your subconscious mind speaks to you most clearly and obviously not through what you choose, but what you *don't* choose. It serves you to look beneath your impulses and inquire—*why would I want it to be this way?* That answer is the beginning of the rest of your life.

05|04|2024

DAY 321

If you promise yourself that they will not stop you,
then they will be able to hold nothing over you.

06/04/2024

DAY 322

When you repeatedly tell yourself that you're going to make it to the life of your dreams, your brain begins to do something magical—it begins to seek out the route. We often look outwards at our lives to tell us who we are, to define us, but in truth it begins in the opposite way. Life affirms what you consistently think. It finds ways to the visions you hold for the longest stretches of time. Your work is not to look around and find the door, but to just believe in what you'll find on the other side.

DAY 323

You can't outrun your own inner knowing. There are some truths that you cannot bargain, justify, or plead away. There are some that stand there like pillars in the center of your soul, waiting until you will acknowledge them, waiting until you will surrender. These truths are the lightning rods that are waiting to strike your life, and the rest is just you getting ready for them; preparing to let them rip open what you had so tightly wound, like a star going supernova and letting its gaseous guts form into new lives, new realities, new existences. That's all you need to look for, at the end of the day—a truth so bold it sets fire to the stories you've told yourself, the safe ways you've chosen to be. There's no logic, there's just ecstatic truth…and that itself is enough. That is enough to build a new life around. That is all any of us are looking for, in the end. Something you love so much no logic can rationalize it down.

DAY 324

Growth is not always predictable. Sometimes, you are clos-est to your greatest breakthroughs while you are moving through shadows so thick, you can barely see an inch ahead of you. Sometimes, the strongest lessons come through quickly because there's something waiting just around the corner, though you do not yet know it. Sometimes, you are exhausted because your attention is being guided to what's draining you, what's taking more than giving. You may think you know where you are on the journey, but you don't always. Healing can be spontaneous, it can be prolonged, it can happen in waves and bits and pieces and in the most unexpected ways. Let it surprise you.

09/04/2024

DAY 325

Beginning again requires you to give up what's *kind of* working on the blind faith that one day, you'll find the things that effortlessly fall into place. Beginning again requires you to let go of what's holding you up so that one day, you'll find the things that let you soar. Beginning again requires you to let go of what's good enough so one day, you can come face-to-face with what's so profoundly, jaw-droppingly, stunning you would never have imagined such a life could exist. Sometimes, you are asked to let go of what's clearly wrong, but more often, you're asked to let go of what's only kind of right, so you can finally find what's an absolute yes.

DAY 326

If you follow the silent guidance within, the part of you that's leading you, intuitively, to the next right step, and the next right step after that, you'll discover that many of the experiences you chalked up to random life encounters were not that at all—they were forming you into the person you were meant to be. You'll look back and realize that every piece of the path was, in some way, an answered prayer—something you wanted, or something you needed, or something inevitable that you had to learn to deal with. Every turn was strengthening you in ways that would have been inconceivable at the time, but here you are, standing, with an inner wisdom deeper than you realize. *One day, you will see the purpose of it all.*

11|04|2024

DAY 327

When was the last time you have simply placed your hand over your heart and felt, truly felt, what was trying to be received by you? When was the last time you really absorbed a kind word, or gesture, when was the last time you really celebrated yourself or acknowledged your progress? Not just letting a thought pass through you, but actually sitting with it, as you are so willing to sit with all of your shortcomings, inconsistencies, and ways in which you'd prefer to be doing better? When was the last time you really gave yourself the credit you deserve?

DAY 328

Nothing will initiate your momentum forward more than realizing how far you have already come. Nothing will more quickly bring you back into the awareness of your own strength.

13/04/2024

DAY 329

When you fear making the wrong turn, you are assuming that life is a fixed set of events that will unfold in accordance with one, singular decision made or not made. This is a gross underestimation of what life really is. Life is a fluid energy, it's consistently reorienting itself around our moment-to-moment stasis. The things you refer to as destined are nothing more than blueprints, set points upon which you will inevitably land not because they are out in the world, but because they are embedded within you. You will, one way or another, express the inner truth inside, but the way that appears on the outside? It's malleable. It's shiftable. It changes by the moment. Yes, there are things inside you that will come to form in one way or another, but you are still a free-willed being on an open-ended planet. Your soul may set the destination, but your brain is navigating your course.

D A Y   3 3 0

It is interesting how often you are in the grips of conviction that you cannot live without something, very often
the same exact thing that you also feel you might not be
able to live with much longer. That sense of dependence is
not a sign that you're meant for that thing, person, or place
and that your consideration of parting with it is an error. It
means that there is some part of your self-concept that is so
wrapped up in its presence it is asking to be released. Begin
there with the mending of the part of you that thinks you
might not survive if not for this singular, transitory element
of your life. Once you are back on steady ground, the answer
of how to move forward will become obvious.

15|04|2024

DAY 331

You would be surprised how much of the past
can be forgiven and forgotten if consistently
different behavior is displayed in the now.

DAY 332

More than a five-year plan, you need a vision for the next hour, the next day, the next week. If you fill your immediate future with the things you know are good for you, the things you know are productive, you will arrive somewhere worthwhile, even if you cannot see beyond that horizon right now. If you learn to live with integrity in the present, one day, you will wake up and realize you are fully immersed in the peace you have been practicing for a very long time.

17/04/2024

DAY 333

When you wake up one day and realize more than half of your life is over, I hope you sleep in and rise to the garden and let your hair fall down by your waist and eat a peach and read a book and drink some tea and let your body be as it is with no thoughts of amendments or adjustments. I hope you have genuine connections and true friends and real love. I hope you will have done all you wanted, I hope you can walk through your house and it feels like home. I hope you will be able to admire all the things you have collected through the years, I hope your hallways are a museum of a life well-lived. I hope you are grateful, I hope you are happy in that peaceful, light-hearted way. I hope you don't consider too long what you might have missed by choosing the life you did. I hope you are satisfied in every way.

18/04/2024

DAY 334

If you're holding yourself back because changing course feels too shameful to bear, imagine if after you took the leap someone met you on the other side and said, *thank goodness, I thought you'd never see the light.* Imagine if that someone was the child inside you.

DAY 335

If you have spent most of your life just trying to survive, things that make your body surge with fear will seem incredibly appealing to you—you will want to be functioning at unrealistically high levels of energy and productivity and development. That is another kind of survival, just with a prettier face. What would it look like to settle into the ease of the day? What would it look like to not get through the hours, but enjoy them? What would it be like to not need extraordinary amounts of energy to accomplish everything you think you need to, and to instead cut that list by a fourth? What would the healing be like if it were about reteaching yourself that there is no guilt in a slow, beautiful, enriching, nourishing life?

20|04|2024

DAY 336

It is either here to teach you how to savor love, or
to remove the block between you and the complete
realization that love is already in the room.

2|| 04 |2024

DAY 337

All change, no matter how minor, requires a period of reac-climation. Your entire being has to get used to functioning within a new frequency, a new dimension you've entered into whether you realize it or not. Your journey will be filled with these new beginnings, and so when you arrive, embrace them. Rest in them. Wash your past clean and start over; let go, let go, let go, and relearn life from this new vantage point, from this new storyline. Let yourself leap into the newness in front of you, and then keep leaping, until you have carved out a sense of home from the once complete unknown.

22/04/2024

DAY 338

Your greatest offering is not always something
you do; most often, it is a person you become.

23l0412024

DAY 339

Your past self does not vanish into nothingness, it is re-leased, often painstakingly and over time. You must cry for every instance in which you closed your throat and repressed what you felt. You must walk each demon to the door. This is really what it means to change—not just to walk away from what is no longer supporting you, but to deconstruct the identity that is no longer equipped to carry you forward, and to build an entirely new one in its place.

DAY 340

Sometimes, the things that feel good aren't really good for you; and sometimes, the things that don't feel good are what you really need. Your life has to be delineated into segments where you engage with both—what soothes and what expands, what nurtures and what fulfills, what is wanted and what is necessary. One without the other will not do, and will not last. You must both strengthen the edges of the life you have already drawn out for yourself and be willing to stretch beyond it—not just outward, but inward. Making way for a deepening, a homecoming.

25|0_H 2024

DAY 341

There will never be a point in your life where you most crave love as when you yourself are void of it, when you have lost love for yourself. Love seems like it comes to us as a fascination, an obsessiveness that convinces us we are indeed divine, but it is in actuality a matching of tone, a way that our outward expression of that divinity meets someone else's, and the two merge into one moving form. The greatness you see in someone else is always an extension of the one you are coming home to inside of yourself; the love we desire outwardly is almost always a calling to more deeply awaken the one inside, and let it be met.

26|04|2024

DAY 342

Prioritize the depth of your connections as opposed to the width of them. It is entirely possible to find yourself in a crowd where you have never felt less alone, less understood. What matters is not how many people you can surround yourself with at any given time, but how much time you spend with the ones who actually see you, who value and prioritize you, who feel like the family you've chosen.

DAY 343

Your purpose is not some mystery you have to unlock or decode; it's something you choose from the elements of your passions and your wants and your inspirations. Your purpose is not something that comes to you out of the blue one day, but something you pull out from deep inside and make your everyday life.

28/04/2024

DAY 344

If you are not yet where you want to be, go find the souls who are standing on your desired horizon. Surround yourself with the people who you admire, who you trust, who you would want to grow to be. Much of your development happens by osmosis, an unconscious acquisition of the traits and thought patterns of those around you. If you are not yet where you want to be, surround yourself with those who are. It will light your path.

29/04/2024

DAY 345

When you fall in love with someone, a stranger becomes a companion. When you nurture a house, it becomes a home. When you practice your gifts, they become a calling. When you steady your mind, you discover an inner river of peace. You are taught to seek, seek, seek outside of yourself, but it's really what you make of the simplest elements of your life that will carry you. What you're looking to find is what you're meant to create.

10/04/2024

DAY 346

The world will begin to see you the way you see yourself, because you will hold yourself differently, you will carry yourself differently, you will speak differently, you will love differently. Your own self-concept is the root of it all, the end and the beginning, the place from which all other relationships stem. You owe yourself your own approval, your own appreciation. You owe it to yourself to become as you've always wanted to be.

DAY 347

It's possible that, at times, your deepest desires are withheld from you, not because they are not meant for you, but because they are so meant for you, you actually have to be ready for them. If you aren't, they'll arrive and pass by swiftly because your container is not wide enough to hold them, to actually see what's in front of you. It's possible that, at times, your deepest desires are being held in trust throughout your most crucial periods of development, not by a universe that's determining if or when your fate should come to you, but by the pacing of your own subconscious mind that knows it's not time to introduce something so consuming, so raw. When you arrive, you will be ready because you are at the helm of your own ship. You are the one walking yourself to your own fate.

DAY 348

What's true for you now will likely not be true forever. You are not the status you hold within this world, you are the awareness behind your eyes that can absorb and interpret and feel into what it sees. You are a field of momentum, you are a visitor to this world, from the next. You are the colors you see and the chords that make you feel something in your chest. You are divine, you are human, nothing and everything all at once. If you learn to define yourself outside the lines, you find a certain kind of freedom. No longer is your worthiness hinging on what you think you have or don't, how you're seen or not. You are not what you're hold-ing, you are the hands that are holding it. That distinction is the difference.

DAY 349

The natural world is the last true thread that connects you to your origin, your source, the space from which you came and will inevitably return. That is why the summer air is so nostalgic to inhale, that is why the trees make you feel rebalanced within yourself, that is why it is so awe-inducing, so healing. It is not separate from you, you separate yourself from it with walls and other materials ascribed to the human condition. It wasn't always that way, though. Nature calls you back to a place you forgot you came from.

DAY 350

The compulsion to prove oneself does not reinforce your sense of self-worth, it slowly diminishes it. It leaves you living on the cusp of constantly finding just *one more thing* to prove you're in the right group, you have the right things, you're on the right path, like everyone else. It does not come from a place where all things beautiful will emerge, it comes from a place that denies that beauty, that assumes it to not be enough. When we seek affirmation from the outside, it's because our first-person experience is being numbed out by the wall we built around our hearts, our feeling capacity. Dismantle it, piece by piece. The more your life is enough for you, the less you will need it to be enough for other people.

05/05/2024

DAY 351

You can also rest into who you're meant to be. You can also breathe into your highest potential future self. You can also lay in the sunlight and it will transform you in its own way. You can make the most important task of the day your cup of tea and it will enlighten you in an important sense. You must release the idea that the only meaningful work is done through effort and forward motion. Sometimes, it's finally staying still that brings your entire universe back into the light.

DAY 352

You will become most concerned with how you are seen when you are not okay with how you are feeling. It is in actuality far simpler to convince the outside world that you are confident and free, and a much deeper process to actually become that way. It requires an unfathomable amount of bravery—there is nothing more trying than letting your pent up pain pass through you, extracting the lessons that need to be learned, and moving on with faith that brighter days are ahead. There is nothing more trying, and nothing more crucial.

07|05|2024

DAY 353

Your job is not to rush the timing.
Rather, to determine the type of person
who will meet it at the doorway.

DAY 354

Maybe that plan you had for your life was built from the pieces of what your child-self thought would keep them safe. You are no longer a child, and you need something more than safety. You need to be set free.

09/03/2024

DAY 355

Not every connection is meant to last forever, and the ending is not a failure. Sometimes, it is a sign of completion. Sometimes, it is a sign of growth. Sometimes, it is a sign of beauty. Sometimes, it is a sign of the truest love of all—the willingness to let someone chase the life that's calling to them.

DAY 356

The delay ensured you arrived just on time. The detour brought you back to what you had thought you lost. The broken heart taught you how to love yourself. The failure awakened your resilience. The night showed you the meaning of the day.

11/05/2024

DAY 357

Your hunger for a more profound and vivid life experience is the clearest sign that you are destined to bring that into existence. It is the truest signal that you are really meant for the level of living that your heart so deeply craves. To have this sort of calling is not always easy—it requires sacrifice, challenge, and growth. It requires vision and self-belief beyond what most could fathom. It requires self-regulation, and it requires strength. It will require everything you've got and give you back more than you ever thought you wanted. It is the meaning of your time here.

DAY 358

I hope you find the courage to change course as often as you need to. I hope you never let your ego keep you on a path you know is not right for you. I hope you understand that life was never meant to move in straight lines, and that most of us live in a state of being too scared to even admit that what we spent so much time constructing around us was built with fragments of foreign, unfamiliar dreams. It takes a lot of heart to release it all into the nothingness and begin again, building a life that is specifically, simply and perfectly your own.

11/05/2024

DAY 359

The journey to what you've asked for can often be unique, and unexpected. There will be twists you never could have anticipated and turns that will make you believe you've gotten it all wrong. More lost than ever, you will assume you are farther from the horizon than you've ever been, but what you don't realize is that you're inching closer by the hour. That is the mystery of being alive. Because of the delay, you arrived right on time. Because of the detour, you were led back to what you thought you had lost. Because of the broken heart, you learned how to love. The sun will set on your life at a very specific hour, and you will be there not a moment before or after. Trust in the labyrinth of experience that you walk through. There is more working beneath the surface than you can understand gazing just above.

D A Y   3 6 0

Your strength, power and happiness is a force that lives within you. It is not in the last chapter, it is not in another person, it is not in one, singular opportunity and whether or not that specific experience comes to be. Your ability to find joy and meaning and radiate pure love is with you always. The rest is a mind game, an activation process, a journey of realizing that everything you were seeking from outside was always waiting for you within. Offer your own love to your own life, learn to see as beautifully as you can. It will change it all, forever. It will lead you to places bigger and more perfect than you ever dared to dream.

15|05|2024

DAY 361

The point is not to be able to think through the complexities of life with more nuance, but to read a book and not have to put it down to check your phone. To be able to sit in nature and let nothing but the clouds above cross your mind. To be at peace with the day as it is. To amend your perception that it is supposed to be different than it is. To be able to accept the moment while still planning for the future—that fine, fine balance. To really experience things more than you just anticipate them. To be in it, all of it, the highs and lows and everything between. To live, finally. To be.

16|05|2024

DAY 362

Life will bring you to your knees. Sometimes with pain, sometimes with beauty, sometimes with both at once. It will weather down your defenses and it will give you opportunities to love. It will disguise miracles in the most ordinary moments. It will bruise your heart until it breaks open. It will teach you, slowly, that it's not out there, it's inside. It's all inside. It will go more slowly than you can bear and more quickly than you can imagine. It will lead you down unexpected turns that twist into destiny, and you will learn to trust. You will learn to believe in the releasing of the layers of illusion that stand between you and the realization of your soul's deepest desires.

17|05|2024

DAY 363

One day, it will be too late. It will be too late to tell them that you love them. It will be too late to begin again. It will be too late to do all of the things you most desire, so do them now, and do them soon, because no tomorrow is a guarantee, it's an assumption we make for our own sanity. We have to believe that there will be more because if there weren't, we'd all be running wild to the things that set our heart ablaze. Maybe that's the problem. Maybe we all need to live a little more in the possibility of today, rather than the promise of tomorrow.

18/05/2024

DAY 364

You should go for it—all of those silly little dreams. All of the little things that keep you up at night and make your heart move a little faster and make you wonder if maybe, just maybe, there's more. The ones that challenge you and follow you and won't let you leave them. Don't die with them still inside.

19|05|2024

DAY 365

I hope you choose a life that inspires you—not spend all of your days just idly imagining that one day, it will mysteriously come to be. I hope you gather the courage and I hope you make decisions you're proud of. I hope you won't get dissuaded when you discover that the smallest steps can feel like the biggest leaps when your heart is afraid. I hope you will dig the most beautiful parts of yourself out from beneath that fear. I hope you won't abandon yourself. I hope you will let the love you want to find within the world begin inside of you. I hope you give yourself credit. I hope you believe in change, because it is guaranteed. I hope you let yourself be guided into destiny. I hope you change your life.

BRIANNA WIEST is the internationally bestselling author of *101 Essays That Will Change The Way You Think*, *The Mountain Is You*, and more. Her books have sold over 1M+ copies worldwide, regularly appear on global bestseller lists, and are currently being translated into 20+ languages. She lives in Big Sur, California.

briannawiest.com
instagram.com/briannawiest
twitter.com/Briannawiest

Please send speaking inquiries to
info@briannawiest.com

Printed in Great Britain
by Amazon